Serial
Killers
of Mexico

Serial
Killers
of Mexico

Chilling Stories of Evil Buried
Beneath the Narcos Drug Wars

Wensley Clarkson

WELBECK

Published by Welbeck
An imprint of Welbeck Non-Fiction Limited,
Part of Welbeck Publishing Group.
Based in London and Sydney
www.welbeckpublishing.com

First published by Welbeck in 2022

A CIP catalogue record for this book is available from the British Library

ISBN
Paperback – 978-1-80279-127-3

Typeset by seagulls.net
Printed in and bound in the UK by CPI Group (UK) Ltd

10 9 8 7 6 5 4 3 2 1

'Do not be afraid;
our fate cannot be taken from us;
it is a gift.'

Dante Alighieri, *Inferno*

THE AUTHOR

Wensley Clarkson has investigated and written about many crimes – including serial killings – across the world for the past 40 years. His research has included prison visits, surveillance operations, police raids and post-mortems. Clarkson's books – published in dozens of countries – have sold more than two million copies. He has also made television documentaries in the UK, US, Australia and Spain and written TV and film screenplays. Clarkson's recent book *Sexy Beasts* – about the Hatton Garden raid – was nominated for a Crime Writers' Association Dagger award.

www.wensleyclarkson.com

DEDICATION

To the innocent victims who found themselves in the wrong place at the wrong time and their heartbroken relatives whose dogged determination brought many of these killers to justice.

CONTENTS

Author's Note   *xiii*

Introduction: Driven to Kill   1

Prologue: Inside the Inferno   5

Chapter 1:   The Strangler of Tacuba   15
             Gregorio Cardenas Hernández

Chapter 2:   The High Priestess of Blood   41
             Magdalena Solís

Chapter 3:   The Sisters of the Inferno   65
             Delfina and María Torres

Chapter 4:   The Juárez Serial Killer   83
             Abdul Latif Sharif

Chapter 5:   The Godfather of Matamoros   99
             Adolfo de Jesús Constanzo

Chapter 6:   The Silent Woman   147
             Juana Dayanara Barraza Samperio

Chapter 7:   The Cannibal Poet   179
             José Luis Calva Zepeda

Chapter 8:   The Sadist Doctor   215
             Raúl Osiel Marroquín Reyes

Chapter 9:   'El Hamburguesa'   237
             David Avendaño Ballina

Chapter 10: The Cartel Assassin   253
             José Rodrigo Aréchiga Gamboa

Chapter 11: The Monsters of Ecatepec   269
             Juan Carlos Hernández and Patricia Martinez

Epilogue: Sicaria Serial Killers   293

Acknowledgements   *301*

AUTHOR'S NOTE

The details of the gruesome murders exposed here have been uncovered thanks to a combination of dogged investigative skills and an ability to put the facts into some semblance of order and readability.

Nothing has been watered down because the primary aim of this book is to emphasise – rather than detract from – the impact of these heinous crimes. However, it was necessary to highlight the disturbing aspects of certain events by using page-turning prose to ensure these true stories flow from a dramatic perspective.

So while all scenes are centred on real circumstances, sometimes dialogue has been expanded. And several names and locations have been changed out of respect for the victims and their families.

I make no apologies in advance to those of you who are squeamish about the graphic scenes described in this book. It would be entirely remiss to avoid the reality of what these serial killers have done and the impact they have had on so many innocent people.

INTRODUCTION: DRIVEN TO KILL

The journey I've been through for this book has helped provide a unique perspective into the serial killers of Mexico, as I have uncovered more hidden secrets about the motivation behind such mass murderers than anything I've written before.

I've focused on the lives of the psychopaths behind these murders because it is the only way to try and understand what drove them to kill in the first place. And in order to get beneath the skin of these characters and find out about the triggers and the tragedies behind their rages, I've had to unpeel their personalities. This meant examining them as human beings rather than heinous killers.

Over the past 35 years, I've encountered male and female serial killers in prisons across the world while researching my books, films and TV documentaries. The majority of them seemed empty, soulless characters who appeared to lack empathy.

They often lived in a state of complete denial when it came to the atrocities they'd committed, even though they faced a one-way trip to the execution chamber or a lifetime in prison. Many of them used their childhoods and life experiences as a protective shield to deflect away from the appalling consequences of their actions.

But I have discovered that many of these individuals were themselves traumatised and unable to process their own appalling experiences in order to avoid the anger and resentment that eventually drove them to murder in the first place. This realisation led me to further investigate the complex nature of these serial killers and how they managed to thrive in Mexico, probably more than any other country on earth.

I would ask readers to occasionally step back from their own emotional perspective and try to look at each case with a fresh eye. To understand the killings, we need to understand each of the killers as individuals. How did they become homicidal maniacs? Why were they more affected by disturbing childhood events than others, who recovered from similar experiences without being psychologically scarred?

The anger and confusion caused by a pivotal event such as child abuse in one's life can be more damaging than the event itself. These disturbing experiences become a subconscious excuse to get revenge on society as these individuals lose the ability to empathise and consider other human beings in real flesh-and-blood terms. This helps them ignore the consequences of their actions which in turn makes it easier for them to take the lives of others. Recognising the red flags before these people become ice-cold killers is more important in the long term than whether they're sentenced to death or serve life in prison.

Until recently, I'd concluded that the twisted yet eloquent serial killer Hannibal Lecter from *The Silence of the Lambs* was a fanciful concoction that in no way related to reality. But as I became more immersed in researching *Serial Killers of Mexico*, I discovered that one of this troubled nation's most notorious such murderers actually helped provide the template for Lecter's character traits. While we may have a single idea of the kind of person who becomes a serial killer, they really do come in all shapes and sizes.

It's not my intention to provide any excuses for these killers, though. I just hope that by uncovering their often sad and tragic lives, it might be possible to prevent others from evolving into being the psychopaths of the future.

PROLOGUE:
INSIDE THE INFERNO

A chilling cross section of serial killers have emerged across Mexico in recent years. Some are psychopathic loners, others are professional narco assassins and many appear to have been driven to kill by their misogyny, which is still, as with many other countries, deeply ingrained in the public consciousness.

But what turned Mexico into what it has become today? Many claim that centuries of colonialism and widespread corruption forced this proud country on to its knees.

While many aspects could be blamed, there is a burning inferno within Mexico's more recent past that's undoubtedly lit the torch that has tainted this entire nation. At least half a million Mexicans have lost their lives as a result of this country's ongoing war with drug cartels over the past three decades. There is nowhere else on earth where professional criminals have so drastically altered the emotional landscape of a country.

These crime gangs have mercilessly held the entire country to ransom, and in many ways have arguably 'normalised' other types of murders by showing citizens that life is cheap. The pressure, both from the international community and from its own government, that is piled on Mexican law enforcement to stamp out the drug cartels has left a huge void that serial killers and other opportunistic killers have gratefully stepped into.

When the drug cartels first emerged in the late 1980s, they were actually seen by many as the twisted saviours of the nation's economy, as Mexico became a thriving transport hub for trillions of dollars' worth of narcotics travelling north into the US.

But Mexico's law-abiding citizens soon found themselves caught in the middle of a cycle of violence, fuelled by these cartels. And as the months turned into years, many would die at the hands of these narco criminals, who were fighting for territory and sending murderous warnings out to the authorities as well as their enemies.

Not even the armed forces have been able to muster enough strength to destroy the narcos in their midst. In recent years, the cartels have forced soldiers and other military units out of their territory thanks to their immense firepower.

The cartels' biggest weapon, though, is money. They've used vast amounts of cash to corrupt almost every corner of public life, often buying off politicians to ensure they can break the law with impunity and bribing army and police chiefs to enable them to continue their illicit activities uninterrupted.

These narcos frequently launch their own recruitment drives specifically targeting Mexico's poorer citizens, who are so often jobless and desperate to feed their families. This has resulted in newly emboldened gangsters who quickly learned that cartel money can buy them just about anything. And if anyone upsets them, they can hire a professional killer for just a few hundred dollars or do the 'job' themselves without fear of arrest or imprisonment.

By the time the Mexican government got around to setting up paramilitary anti-narco units in the mid 1990s, it was already too late. They could do little but stand by and watch as citizens were obliged to accept the drug cartels in their midst or pay the ultimate price.

Today, Mexico has many modern cities that appear to be thriving, at least on the surface. But every one of them is under the control of a drug cartel. That even includes Mexico City itself. And the country's fat cat politicians continue to condemn the narcos in public, while many still accept their black money behind everyone's back.

Serial killers of Mexico have been further aided by the police's antiquated investigative techniques and underfunding, which means many police officers can't be bothered to launch investigations into murders committed by strangers, as they end up being too difficult to solve.

In Mexico, law enforcement officers also often lack large-scale computerised databases, which would make it possible to connect many of the serial killings that have swept through this damaged nation for so long.

DNA fingerprints – which have helped solve so many serious crimes in more developed parts of the world for almost 40 years – were not even fully utilised in Mexico until less than two decades ago.

In addition to this, a regressive macho attitude inside much of the force has led to an underestimation of many female serial killers, who are given belittling and sexist nicknames such as 'La Flaca', meaning 'The Skinny One', 'La Gorda', 'The Fat One', and 'La Pequeña', 'The Little One'. The clear inference was and still is that their gender made them less threatening than their male equivalents, despite committing multiple murders.

Mexican police, like many forces around the world, have also become notorious in recent years for making arrests, regardless of guilt or innocence. According to sources, over-zealous officers regularly force confessions out of innocent citizens suspected of being serial killers. This, importantly to a discussion about serial killers, enables the guilty to continue committing their heinous crimes.

Mexico's government also tries to avoid publicising its sky-high murder rate because politicians and public officials are embarrassed by the country's global reputation as a deadly, feral narco state. Independent investigators in Mexico have even uncovered evidence that some individual serial killing cases have been deliberately covered up by police, who are embarrassed by their failure to solve such a string of murders.

Criminologists believe that this 'perfect storm' of crime and police failures, all fuelled by Mexico's deadly narco wars, has helped this nation become an ideal hunting ground for many of the most bizarre and bloodthirsty serial killers in criminal history.

'If I was a serial killer looking for new victims I'd head over the border to Mexico because life is cheap there and the cops have got so much other shit to investigate, they don't bother with random killings,' one former DEA officer explained.

* * *

A dark line connects many of the serial killings featured in this book with Mexico's most contentious religious sect. The god of death – Santa Muerte – dominates the beliefs of many poorer Mexicans, who believe her powers can help them find immense riches. Santa Muerte's nicknames include 'Flaquita' ('Skinny Girl') or 'Huesuda' ('Bony Lady') which sum up the ominous shadow of death that looms over much of this country.

Images of Santa Muerte often appear on makeshift road-side shrines, usually in the poorest neighbourhoods and city slums. She's a skeleton dressed in a loose robe and carrying a scythe, illuminated by candles and prayer cards. These shrines contain cigarettes, alcohol and spare change, which people are offering to Santa Muerte in exchange for her protection.

Santa Muerte evolved from this nation's staunch Catholicism combined with pre-Colombian and African ancestry. The Catholic Church itself has refused to officially recognise Santa Muerte but in many ways this has made her even more popular with followers. Santa Muerte has even been used by some serial killers to hypnotise people into carrying out the slaughter of many innocents, as is highlighted by several cases in this book.

In 2003, Mexico's government actually added Santa Muerte to its list of registered religions. But in 2005, politicians reversed this decision and decreed it as a fraudulent movement.

Mexican officials then ordered the bulldozing of thousands of shrines devoted to Santa Muerte across the nation. But none of this put off the God of Death's millions of followers. They continued to insist Santa Muerte would one day answer all their prayers by rewarding them with real love and great riches.

Others have dubbed Santa Muerte as the serial killer's ultimate friend, as followers have been accused of giving her disciples a twisted licence to kill those who do not share their beliefs.

In July 2020, a 10-year-old boy called Martin Ríos disappeared from Nacozari de García, a small copper mining community near Hermosillo, in the Mexican state of Sonora. At first, the case got little attention. Martin's mother and her boyfriend told state police that friends had said they'd seen the boy begging on the streets of a nearby town called Agua Prieta. Officers promised to go and fetch Martin, but by the time they had travelled to Agua Prieta, the child had disappeared.

Then in March 2011, another 10-year-old called Jesús Martínez disappeared from Nacozari de García, where missing Martin had come from. It emerged that both children had been frequent visitors to the home of Jesús's step-grandmother, 44-year-old Silvia Meraz, who was renowned locally as a Santa Muerte priestess.

Meraz and her family lived in a run-down house on the edge of Nacozari de García. Authorities were already suspicious about them because of the large number of apparent strangers visiting Meraz's home. The police were convinced the house was being used for prostitution but had never been able to prove this. Eventually, the long-standing cases of the two missing boys provided them with an excuse to finally raid the property in March 2012.

Shocked investigators quickly uncovered the remains of Jesús Martínez buried beneath the dirt floor of one of Meraz's daughters' bedrooms. Police immediately arrested Meraz and seven other members of the household: her father, her son and daughter-in-law, three daughters and her boyfriend. They were all followers of Santa Muerte.

Then two family members confessed to police that the body of another missing boy, Martin Ríos, was hidden on the family property. As investigators uncovered his remains, they also stumbled on the makeshift grave of Cleotilde Romero Pacheco, a 55-year-old woman who'd been friends with Meraz before disappearing from her home in nearby Nacozari in 2009.

All three of the victims' throats and wrists had been slit. And the two missing children's bodies had been decapitated. A police forensic team matched all the victims' blood to smears on an altar dedicated to Santa Muerte that stood in the main living room.

Meraz later told investigators that she and her family believed that the blood sacrifices of their victims would ensure they got rich, a belief apparently based on the spiritual doctrine of Santa Muerte.

All eight suspects were eventually charged with first-degree homicide, robbery, corrupting minors, illegal burial and conspiracy. One of the accused was a 15-year-old girl. The suspects admitted to prosecutors that the murders occurred during candlelit Santa Muerte rituals held late at night.

One investigator later explained: 'They sliced open the victims' veins and – while they were still alive – the killers waited for them to bleed to death before collecting their blood in a container.' Ringleader Silvia Meraz even admitted to reporters during one subsequent court appearance: 'We all agreed to do it. Supposedly she [one of the victims] was a witch or something.'

Meraz was sentenced to a total of 180 years in prison for the murders. The other cult members were sentenced to 60 years in prison, while her 15-year-old daughter was sent to a youth detention centre.

They say death is cheap in Mexico, especially if you come from the poverty-stricken neighbourhoods where corpses often lie untouched on roadsides while people and cars pass by, without giving a second glance. It's a dangerous country where death and destruction dominate the lives of many normal, law-abiding citizens.

Welcome to the Serial Killers of Mexico …

CHAPTER ONE

THE STRANGLER OF TACUBA
GREGORIO CARDENAS HERNÁNDEZ

Gregorio Cardenas Hernández was a small, shy eight-year-old with a tendency to look down whenever anyone talked to him. Goyo – short for Gregorio – also suffered from severe health problems, which led to him one day defecating in his trousers in the middle of class.

No one realised what had happened until the other pupils pointed out the pungent smell. Little Goyo burst into tears as they laughed out loud and called him 'shit pants' over and over again. His teacher looked irritated and ordered him out of the classroom.

As Goyo got up, with difficulty as his soiled trousers were stuck to his chair, he slipped in his own excrement and smashed his forehead on the corner of a desk. No one – not even his teacher – tried to help Goyo get up. Instead, his classmates watched as he struggled back on his feet. With his eyes crunched up with pain and trepidation, he hesitantly stumbled out of the classroom sobbing.

A few minutes later, another teacher heard Goyo crying in a toilet cubicle. He was too afraid to come out. His trousers were so badly soiled, he couldn't put them back on. The same teacher eventually persuaded Goyo to open the cubicle door, wrapped a towel around him and escorted him along the busy school corridor as more schoolchildren poked fun at him.

Goyo was ordered by the school's headmaster to wait outside his office until his mother Vicenta Hernández came to pick him up. Goyo later recalled that no one else said another word to him as he sat there shivering in the flimsy towel.

When Goyo's mother Vicenta finally arrived at the school to collect him, she seemed irritated. She hadn't even brought him a change of clothes, so he faced more humiliation as his mother pulled him along by the hand back along the main school corridor towards the front exit of the school.

Goyo later claimed that what happened that day at school in 1920s Mexico City was mainly his mother's fault. She'd been too ashamed to tell the school in the first place that her young son had a brain disease known as encephalitis, which meant he couldn't control his bowels.

But it wasn't just at school where Goyo faced endless humiliation. On the streets of the Tacuba district of Mexico City, where he lived with his family, Goyo constantly felt people staring at him because of his extremely spindly, long, skinny arms and the fact one of his legs was shorter than the other, which meant he had a distinct limp.

From a young age, Goyo preferred reading and painting to playing with other children. He had an extremely intelligent, analytical mind and lived more inside his own head than anywhere else.

His mother, Vicenta Hernández, was the one person in his life he should have had a close relationship with. However, she wasn't very loving towards him, rarely showing him affection, and was so embarrassed by his physical appearance that she'd often make him walk behind her when they were out on the busy city streets.

Vicenta's relatives and friends later recalled that she snapped at Goyo much of the time and ordered him around as if he were an irritating pet dog, rather than someone she gave birth to. But back home, away from the prying eyes of her rich friends and family, Vicenta insisted Goyo slept in her bed with her when her husband was away on business, which occurred frequently.

Goyo later claimed that his relationship with his mother was so suffocatingly inconsistent that he spent much of his time trying to avoid her, which meant being alone in his bedroom or in the backyard of the family's large detached house entertaining himself.

Bored and curious about the world, Goyo became fascinated with death from a young age. And with no one to talk to about it, he devised his own unique 'experiments' to satisfy that interest.

It began by throttling animals, including rabbits, mice and rats, just to see how much they suffered when they were dying. He later recalled that he saw each death as the culmination of a scientific experiment. He felt no malice towards the animals themselves but felt, to feed his own curiosity, he needed to take their lives.

None of Goyo's other family members cared about the way he inflicted pain on innocent animals and then avidly watched them die. To them, he was just 'Little Goyo' – a strange, bespectacled, eccentric child.

In the wake of the incident at school, Goyo's mother solved her son's problems by insisting he wore a thick cotton nappy to school. He hated wearing the nappy because it was so bulky it made his trousers look a strange shape. He was certain his classmates could tell he had it on, although no one actually said anything to him in class, apart from still calling him 'shit pants' over and over again.

At home, Goyo didn't dare complain to his mother. She only cared that he got good marks in class and threatened him with punishment if he didn't.

Goyo achieved high academic grades at school mainly because he had a high IQ and few diversions at home, unlike most other children. No one took any interest in him once class was over. He spent most of his time alone in the school playground and most afternoons he'd settle down in a corner of the school library to complete his homework before he left for the day. Therefore Goyo's teachers were not surprised when he passed all his exams with flying colours and earned himself a place at the National Autonomous University of Mexico (UNAM).

He soon earned himself a reputation as one of the brightest science students of his academic year. The powerful fuel giant Petróleos Mexicanos (PEMEX) awarded Goyo a cash scholarship to cover all his living and academic costs while he trained to be a research scientist and they also encouraged him to begin developing new products for the company.

Still living at home with his mother, Vicenta, Goyo continued to appear to the outside world as her favourite, beloved son. But visitors to the house at that time noticed that she treated 21-year-old Goyo as if he were still a child, no more than 10 years old.

Goyo remained the dutiful son by always helping his mother with the housework. And when he began earning a proper salary at PEMEX, he gave half of it straight to his mother. Goyo's other brothers and sisters had long since left home, but he felt unable to leave his mother on her own because he knew only too well how vulnerable and lonely she was.

Most evenings after work, Goyo would complete his home chores and then devote himself to painting and playing the piano. All the while, he also continued carrying out gruesome experiments on animals. These took place in a shed he had built in the backyard of the family home.

Goyo's world revolved around the house and the PEMEX laboratory where he worked in the centre of Mexico City. He was painfully shy with girls and awkward with his peers. Busying himself at home was a useful diversion from the pressure of having to socialise.

Despite his sheltered life, and like most young people, Goyo was sexually curious, but he struggled to understand the mere notion of dating girls. In general, he was far too shy and unconfident to approach or speak to them.

In the end, though, he was so driven by a determination to have a 'proper' relationship that he plucked up the courage to chat up a girl called Sabina González Lara, whom he met in a local cafe.

Instead of taking his time courting her, Goyo fell instantly head over heels in love with Sabina after that first meeting. Sabina later recalled that Goyo appeared so terrified of being rejected that his solution was to immediately ask her to marry him.

She later realised he did it in order to guarantee she couldn't ditch him. Despite being surprised by his sudden request, Sabina agreed as she liked Goyo. She later said she trusted him because he seemed so gentle, considerate and thoughtful.

In preparation for their marriage, Goyo rented them a plush apartment at 20 Mar del Norte Street, in the district of Tacuba close to his mother's house, and insisted Sabina didn't have to get a job because he would provide for them both.

Sabina later said she felt uneasy as soon as they'd got married because it had happened so quickly. However Goyo continually insisted he was madly in love with her so Sabina didn't want to disappoint him. But as soon as he returned to work, she found herself in their apartment feeling lonely, deflated and bewildered as to what she was doing there in the first place. She also began noticing that Goyo regularly wet their bed at night.

Goyo didn't help matters by refusing to talk to Sabina about it when he got home from work that evening. And as the days turned into weeks, Sabina began to long for a life of freedom again. Besides his bladder problems, the apartment had started to feel like a prison so she began meeting friends during the daytime while Goyo was at work. They all told her she'd been mad to get married so quickly and when they heard about her husband's bed-wetting, they rolled their eyes in disgust.

Less than a month into the marriage, Sabina noticed that her new husband had once again wet the bed when she went to make it after he'd left for work. It was the final straw. She packed all her bags up that same morning and left the apartment. She left him a note explaining that she had fallen in love with another man. It wasn't true but she needed an excuse to leave him.

When Goyo read it when he got home that evening, he smashed up the apartment in a fit of fury. He later admitted being thankful that Sabina hadn't been there at the time, as he felt like she might have got seriously hurt.

Following that disastrous, short-lived marriage, Goyo began hiring sex workers. But – rather than face the humiliation of sleeping with them in a brothel where someone might see him – he found teenage streetwalkers prepared to come to the rented apartment he'd once shared with his new wife. He preferred them to be under 20 because, at that young, impressionable age, he believed they wouldn't humiliate him or treat him like some sort of circus freak because of his disability. He also 'felt safer' if the women were on his 'territory' when they slept together.

On one boiling hot day in August 1942, Goyo – now aged 24 – paid for the services of 16-year-old prostitute María de los Ángeles González, who called herself 'Bertha' and walked the streets of the Tacuba area close to his home.

Within minutes of arriving at Goyo's ground floor apartment, he became extremely nervous about the prospect of having sex with Bertha, even though he had just initiated the situation. He later said he was confused by his sexual urges because they were so overwhelming that he made decisions he later regretted.

But despite his nerves, they eventually managed to start having sex, although Goyo defecated before he achieved an orgasm. Bertha was so disgusted she screamed and yelled at him to clear it up and refused to help him do so.

As Goyo stripped the sheets off the bed, Bertha mockingly accused him of being 'shit scared' of her and then laughed at her own insensitive joke. Goyo gritted his teeth and tried to ignore her as he dropped the badly soiled sheets into the bath. But Bertha continued humiliating Goyo. She even demanded he pay her the full fee plus a generous tip to compensate for what had happened.

Goyo tried to contain his anger towards Bertha with careful breathing exercises he'd learned from a colleague at work. But as he soaked the soiled sheets in the bath, she continued humiliating him. He eventually got up, slowly walked up behind her, placed his hands around her neck and squeezed so tightly that she fell unconscious to the floor within seconds.

Goyo calmly ripped a cord from an overhanging curtain, straddled her limp body and wrapped the cord around her neck. Then he began pulling it tighter and tighter until he was certain she was dead. Goyo later recalled that the moment after the killing was the first time in his entire life that he was actually able to achieve sexual satisfaction.

Afterwards, Goyo carefully and methodically buried the teenage girl in the back garden of his apartment. Then he headed round to his mother's house, as he didn't feel like spending the night alone.

Vicenta was delighted to see her son and insisted he shared her bed that night. Nothing sexual happened between them but Goyo later said that as he lay there he got an erection thinking about how he'd just ended that young girl Bertha's life.

Goyo kept thinking about the expression on her face, as her bulging eyes virtually popped out of their sockets while he squeezed the life out of her. In his head, he had no doubt that Bertha deserved to die for humiliating him. He would claim in interviews that he wished he'd done the same thing to all those children who'd laughed at him when he defecated in his trousers in the classroom all those years earlier.

A few days after the incident, Goyo hired the services of another young prostitute, a 14-year-old girl who was known as Erendira on the streets of Tacuba. He feared that, in order to achieve his own sexual climax again, this girl would also most likely have to die. But Goyo managed to convince himself that this time he could achieve what he wanted without having to commit actual murder.

Goyo became so obsessed with having 'normal sex' with Erendira that he began sweating profusely as they tried to do it. When she looked up and saw the way his eyes had glazed over, she started resisting. Infuriated that he was being rejected, he became very tense, which gave him an immense headache. He decided the only way to stop it getting worse was to rape her.

Afterwards Goyo apologised profusely, but the girl accused him of being 'a creep' and demanded her money. She also threatened to tell her brothers what had happened and said that they'd come round and 'sort him out'.

Erendira's words cut through Goyo like a knife. As she continued berating him over what had happened, once again he tried to breathe slowly and deeply, not wanting to respond. But that didn't work and eventually he got up, took the same piece of cord from earlier out of a drawer and walked up behind Erendira. He quickly looped it around her neck and pulled so hard that the cord tore through her flesh.

Later that night, Goyo buried teenager Erendira's body in a shallow grave in the garden alongside Bertha's corpse. Goyo later admitted he knew that killing both women was wrong, but his actions had unleashed a need for sexual satisfaction like no other feeling he had ever experienced.

A couple of weeks later, Goyo murdered 16-year-old prostitute Rosa Reyes by also tying that same cord around her neck and strangling her after she refused to have sex with him. Her body was buried in the garden alongside his first two victims.

Rosa Reyes's murder was followed two weeks later by the killing of yet another 16-year-old sex worker. Again, she was strangled and buried in the garden.

A few days later, Goyo approached a prostitute on the street near his home. She later recalled how she was about to go with him when an expensive car slowed down alongside them. The prostitute glanced at Goyo and then at the wealthy businessman in his big car and chose the other client instead.

That older customer apparently ended up taking her to Tequisquiapan, in the state of Querétaro, for a weekend break.

Having got not only a holiday, but also avoided almost certain death, the same woman later described herself as being 'the luckiest whore in Mexico City'.

The following day, Goyo was driving along a street in the district of Tacuba when he noticed 21-year-old Graciela Arias Ávalos walking on the pavement. The difference here was that Graciela was not a sex worker. Goyo knew her from when they'd both been chemistry students at university. Goyo stopped his car, rolled down the window and asked Graciela to have an ice cream with him.

The pair ended up having dinner together in a restaurant that evening. Seemingly believing this could be something romantic, when Graciela got into Goyo's car in an empty, badly lit street afterwards, he tried to kiss her. She slapped him in the face to stop him and told him she didn't find him attractive.

Goyo later said he was so shocked by her rejection, that for a few moments he gripped the steering wheel as tightly as possible to stop himself attacking her. He stated that she continued lecturing him in the car, so he took one hand off the steering wheel and grappled around for a length of cord he kept in the pocket of the driver's door.

Still staring ahead through the windscreen, Goyo held the cord tightly in one hand and tried once again to resist the temptation to hurt her. It seemed to be working until she announced she no longer wanted a ride home. He took his other hand off the steering wheel and leaned across to where she was sitting and grabbed her by the neck.

With one deft movement, he wrapped the cord around Graciela's neck and stared intensely into her face, strangling her so tightly that her head almost separated from the rest of her body. Afterwards, Goyo put her corpse in the boot of his car and drove back to his apartment.

Later that same evening, Goyo removed Graciela's body from his car and carried it over his shoulder into his apartment wrapped in a rug. He laid her corpse carefully on his bed, spread her legs apart and then, for the following four hours, raped it. When he'd finished, Goyo buried the remains in the same part of the garden that already contained the corpses of the other women he'd killed.

While all of Goyo's previous victims had come from poverty-stricken backgrounds, Graciela's father was a renowned criminal lawyer called Manuel Arias Córdova. He had a close relationship with the Mexico City police, as well as the government's Public Ministry.

So within hours of Graciela's disappearance, Señor Córdova put the police under immense pressure to find his missing daughter. More than a dozen police officers began scouring the Tacuba district where she'd last been seen. They eventually came across two witnesses who'd seen Graciela getting into a car driven by eccentric local scientist Goyo on the afternoon she'd gone missing.

Investigators immediately switched their enquiries to the Mar del Norte area of Tacuba, where Goyo lived in that apartment close to his mother Vicenta's home. None of Goyo's neighbours had seen him that day, but a couple of them told police that they'd grown increasingly suspicious of Goyo's noisy late night garden excavation work.

One revealed he'd confronted Goyo about those strange activities as he left for work one morning. But Goyo had brushed off the man's questions by insisting no one had even been inside his apartment. Another resident in the apartment block told detectives she'd heard women's screams coming from Goyo's apartment on several occasions over the previous few months.

Goyo soon heard about the police enquiries and became convinced it was only a matter of time before detectives came knocking on his door. Believing he was in need of urgent psychiatric help, Goyo committed himself as a voluntary patient into a local sanatorium. It was run by a world-renowned mental health expert called Dr Gregorio Oneto Barenque.

Goyo later claimed he was relieved to have got himself off the streets and into treatment as he knew he had to stop killing any more innocent women. He was examined in the mental health facility by resident psychiatrist Dr Quiroz Cuarón, who concluded that Goyo had an acutely neurotic personality, evolutionary neurosis, organ neurosis, narcissism and seemed obsessed with anal sadistic eroticism.

Dr Cuarón also insisted on contacting the police to inform them of Goyo's decision to commit himself. Detectives, under immense pressure from the latest victim's well-connected father, assumed Goyo was trying to avoid arrest and spoke to a local judge about getting a warrant for his arrest.

The judge issued a warrant after rejecting the mental health experts' prognosis on the basis that Goyo had to be sane because he'd graduated with a top-class honours degree. The judge also noted that Goyo showed no external signs of actual insanity.

On 7 September 1942, a heavily armed police unit detained Goyo inside the clinic and he was taken in a convoy directly to a cell at Mexico City police headquarters.

Back in the small garden of Goyo's apartment, police uncovered the shallow grave of a teenage girl they presumed to be a missing 16-year-old called Raquel González, whose disappearance had been reported to them a few weeks earlier. However, later that same day, Raquel walked into police headquarters to announce she was very much alive and had run away with a boyfriend, which was why she'd gone missing.

It was only many years later that police were able to establish that the first corpse they'd found was that of the young prostitute known only as Erendira. No one ever claimed her body or reported her disappearance. And after excavation of the rest of the garden, the other corpses were also found.

During a 10-hour-long interview by detectives at Mexico City police headquarters, Goyo admitted to investigators he'd not only killed the four women whose bodies were buried in his garden but he'd also had sex with his victims after they'd died.

When one of the officers interrogating Goyo asked him why he'd begun killing women in the first place, he explained about his previous marriage and how the relationship had broken down when his wife ran off with another man. Goyo told detectives that his wife's adulterous behaviour had turned him into a woman hater and this had directly led to him murdering the women.

Goyo also claimed to investigators that he'd carried out chemical experiments on the corpse of each victim, injecting them with a variety of substances to see how their corpses responded. This later turned out to be a lie. Goyo cleverly wanted to ensure his lawyers gave the impression in court that he was a mad scientist, rather than a cold-blooded killer.

The press in Mexico City immediately nicknamed Goyo 'The Strangler of Tacuba' and he was moved from his police station cell to Mexico's largest prison El Palacio Negro de Lecumberri to await his trial.

Back at Goyo's family home, his sister was devastated by the allegations that her brother was a serial killer. Just a few weeks after his arrest, she died of an acute myocardial infarction, which doctors said was directly related to the stress she had been subjected to.

Goyo's trial was heard relatively quickly after he made it clear to investigators that he'd be pleading guilty to all four murders he'd been accused of. The judge sentenced Goyo to life in prison, the only appropriate jail term for the crimes he'd committed.

Prison was expected to be a rude awakening for the shy, well-educated, middle-class Goyo, who found himself in jail with some of Mexico's most dangerous killers. Journalists and criminals alike predicted he'd end up being murdered by other inmates in revenge for the way he'd killed those innocent young women.

However, most prisoners grew to like Goyo, despite the brutality of his crimes. Goyo showed particular compassion towards inmates who couldn't afford lawyers to prove their innocence. Many of them weren't properly registered in the prison, so their families had no idea they were even locked up.

Goyo helped these inmates – many of whom were illiterate – to write letters and contact lawyers to represent them, and this further improved his relationship with many prisoners and staff. He also attended psychiatric sessions and regularly received visits from his family. He was even permitted by prison authorities to plant a tree inside his cell, which had so many shelves on the walls brimming with books that many inmates said it resembled a university lecturer's office.

During a short bout of illness inside Lecumberri prison, Goyo was so charming to the prison nurses in the infirmary that prison authorities insisted Goyo was given a special licence to go out on day release. Unfortunately, on that sunny day in the middle of 1947, Goyo failed to return after a visit to his family. He'd fled to the city of Oaxaca, hundreds of miles south-east of Mexico City.

Goyo's escape was seen by many as a huge embarrassment for the authorities, who'd kept their decision to award him day release secret. Many claimed he'd been given preferential treatment because of his family's connections to certain powerful Mexican politicians.

As police launched a nationwide manhunt for the notorious serial killer, several members of the public told the media that Goyo was harmless and authorities should leave him in peace and not bother sending him back to jail. Others warned that Goyo was a chilling and extremely dangerous psychopath whose crimes were classic examples of the type of gender violence that was typical of that era in Mexico.

Some demanding his capture publicly linked Goyo's necrophilia to legendary criminals of the past including Jack the Ripper, Bluebeard and the notorious Vampire of Düsseldorf, all of whom were said to have an obsession with having sex with dead bodies.

Goyo later said he was surprised by the media response to his escape and insisted he'd never thought of himself as being a danger to the public. For a few days he wrestled with his conscience while on the run before surrendering to police. And Goyo's actions made him appear very different from so-called 'normal' killers who would have stayed on the lam for as long as they could.

On Goyo's return to Lecumberri prison, he was greeted as a hero by other inmates impressed by the way his escape from jail had humiliated many public officials. All this helped fuel Goyo's bizarre new status as a national treasure, who just happened to be a mass murderer.

Back in Mexico City, there were allegations that several copycat killers were imitating Goyo's methodical homicidal habits now that he'd managed to make murder look glamorous. A pornographic film based on his story was even made, which became a box office hit inside Mexico.

Back in prison, Goyo settled down and wrote three books, as well as agreeing to be regularly psychoanalysed by some of the country's top mental health experts. These experts would claim that Goyo was a classic example of a psychopath.

Goyo was permitted by prison authorities to study psychiatry and law while inside, and also improved his piano playing, wrote a lot of poetry, and began a pen friendship with a woman called Gerarda Valdés Cuicas, who'd been following Goyo's case ever since his original arrest.

Less than six months after this unlikely long-distance relationship began, Goyo and Gerarda married. She adopted her husband's first surname following their marriage and the couple were even permitted conjugal visits during Goyo's ongoing incarceration.

When newspapers exposed the conjugal visits, Mexican women's groups accused prison authorities of cheapening the memory of his victims. But Goyo's marriage convinced other members of the public that he was much less dangerous than most of the convicted murderers incarcerated with him.

One of the nurses Goyo had earlier charmed inside prison insisted during a radio phone-in interview at the time that Goyo was not a violent individual. She described him as 'a kind and good person'.

* * *

For the following 30 years, Goyo proved himself to be a model prisoner, even earning a diploma in criminal law after completing a correspondence training course. All this helped Goyo to qualify as a 'practitioner of law' which meant he could legally process appeals and even oversee case reviews for other inmates, including those poorer ones whom he'd always gone out of his way to help.

Goyo eventually defended several prisoners inside Lecumberri prison whom he believed to be innocent. Many of these inmates would never have found the justice they sought without his involvement, as they'd not been able to afford lawyers.

On 1 September 1975, Lecumberri prison was closed down by authorities because it was in such a bad state of disrepair. No one raised an eyebrow when veteran inmate Goyo helped administer the safe transferral of prisoners to the newly constructed Tepepan prison, in Xochimilco.

By this time, he was renowned as a rehabilitated character on all fronts.

Less than a year later – on 18 August 1976 – Goyo was awarded an early release because of what authorities described as his 'exemplary behaviour'.

By this time, Goyo and the wife he'd married in prison had five children; 20-year-old Miguel Ángel, 18-year-old Julio César, 16-year-old Gustavo, 15-year-old Marcos and 13-year-old Guadalupe. They all used the surname Cárdenas Valdés after their father.

Two days after his release from prison, Goyo informed reporters gathered outside his family home in a wealthy suburb of Mexico City in a slow, quiet voice that the prison regime he'd served under was the most humane in the history of Mexico. He insisted authorities had 'a real interest in those who have committed crimes, to try to rehabilitate them'.

Goyo himself was being treated more like a celebrity than a serial killer. He and his family were even able to afford to move into a larger family house in an exclusive district of Mexico City. The interior walls of the colonial-style property were covered with many of the pictures Goyo had painted during his 30 years inside prison.

At this time, Goyo's wife Gerarda granted one exclusive interview to a female newspaper reporter, during which she insisted that her serial killer husband was a 'normal, understanding and loving man'.

She explained: 'Despite all that we have suffered from the imprisonment of my husband and everything that has been said, I have no grudge against anyone.'

His wife also revealed plans for the couple to marry 'properly' in a church, now that her husband was no longer in prison.

She told the same reporter: 'Thus we will be meeting all the requirements that God sends, because we are both Catholic and for now we are only civilly married. Anyway, I still love him.'

Goyo made a special point of regularly returning to prison to see inmates and staff. He told one reporter he still enjoyed playing cards with them, as well as chess.

In Mexico City's rich, upper-crust society, Goyo continued to be feted almost like a film star. Some of Goyo's wealthy supporters even began insisting that mass killers like Goyo were not real killers. They quoted an academic paper he'd written on mental health that seemed to excuse the killings he'd committed.

But Goyo was seen by others as manipulating rich and entitled people with his charm and intelligence, to the point where they were in a state of complete denial about what he'd done.

Then highly respected Mexico City criminologist Alfonso Quiroz Cuarón – who'd first examined Goyo when he committed himself before his arrest – publicly claimed that Goyo's homicidal behaviour had been caused by the encephalitis he'd suffered during his childhood. This, insisted Cuarón, had led to an infection in Goyo's nervous system which left him in such pain that his tolerance levels were non-existent.

There were also male chauvinists inside Mexican society at that time who believed that Goyo's victims were simply 'loose women', who deserved to die for living 'immoral lives'.

Several prominent politicians began putting pressure on the then president of Mexico, Luis Echeverría Álvarez, to award Goyo a 'presidential pardon'. Despite furious protests by women's rights groups, it was eventually granted.

After the president had granted his pardon, Secretary of the Interior of the Mexican government, Señor Mario Moya Palencia, invited Goyo to deliver a speech to the Mexican parliament's Chamber of Deputies. Many politicians insisted that Goyo deserved this opportunity because he was a unique example of how prisoners could be properly reintegrated into society.

Goyo opened his speech by telling the legislators: 'This is one of the most emotional moments of my life.'

He pledged to use his skills as a lawyer to continue to defend prisoners too poor to pay for their own defence attorneys. At the end of the speech, Goyo was given a standing ovation.

But his speech sparked outrage among many ordinary Mexicans, especially women, who described Goyo's murders as blatant femicide, which had been twisted by public opinion into being a supposed 'inspiration for Mexicans'.

Armed with his presidential pardon, Goyo was permitted to enrol at Mexico City's Universidad Nacional Autónoma de México (UNAM) to study political science, despite being a convicted mass murderer. Officials at the university repeatedly insisted to the media that Goyo had already 'paid his debt to society'.

In late 1982, Goyo was awarded the title of Bachelor of Criminal Law after several politicians appealed to the rectory of the university where Goyo had studied that he should be accredited with the title because he'd achieved one of the highest grades ever recorded in his final examinations.

Meanwhile Goyo's case was inspiring numerous plays, films and TV programmes. Goyo himself attended the Helénico theatre showing a play called *El Criminal de Tacuba* which centred on his real-life killings.

Goyo said afterwards he wasn't happy about the way his personality had been portrayed in the play. He eventually sued the producers and writers claiming they had libelled him. Incredibly, a judge eventually awarded Goyo eight million old pesos (£45,000) in compensation. Following this, Goyo told reporters he still felt very vulnerable to criticism in Mexico City, so he and his family left and relocated to Los Angeles, California.

Goyo used the compensation money from his libel case to purchase a big house in one of the city's wealthiest areas for his wife and numerous children and grandchildren. The family insisted to curious Californians that Goyo was an exemplary character, who'd shown himself to be an excellent father and friend.

Goyo much preferred his lower profile in Los Angeles, where film stars made many more headlines than him. His new-found life of relative obscurity came to an end on 2 August 1999, when he died of kidney complications aged 84.

These days – more than two decades after Goyo's death – he is still considered by many as being a 'groundbreaking psychopath'. Not only was he a serial killer before the term was even invented but, in spite of his heinous crimes, his charm and intelligence undoubtedly helped him talk his way back into society, which continues to raise questions about his sanity.

But the biggest question of all surrounding Goyo's crimes has never properly been answered. Can a serial killer ever put his murderous instincts behind him?

There are some in Mexico who are still convinced that Goyo killed other women following his release from prison. But whatever the truth of the matter, Goyo has gone down in criminal folklore as one of the real-life serial killers who inspired the fictional creation of Hannibal Lecter. A man whose intelligence and charm never quite aligned with the heinousness of his crimes.

CHAPTER TWO

THE HIGH PRIESTESS OF BLOOD

MAGDALENA SOLÍS

When Magdalena Solís was born, back in 1947, the village of Tamaulipas in Mexico and its 50 residents were the epitome of the phrase 'dirt poor'. The village had no electricity and the water supply came directly from a polluted nearby river and a horse and cart was the most common form of transport. The life expectancy of villagers was just 33 years of age.

Tamaulipas remained so cut off from the rest of the world when Magdalena was growing up during the 1950s that the majority of residents didn't even know what a television was, let alone own one. Magdalena Solís and her younger brother Eleazar dealt with this extreme isolation by helping each other through their difficult childhood.

Magdalena's own father slept with her on a regular basis and other relatives sexually abused Eleazar. These family assailants claimed they attacked the children because they were exorcising the Devil from them both. The two siblings were also forced to drink the blood of chickens killed on a makeshift altar in the backyard of the family home. After such occasions, Magdalena and Eleazar would often end up back in a bedroom being assaulted yet again.

Their mother always looked the other way because she knew what would happen if she ever dared say something to her husband and his relatives. As a result, Magdalena and Eleazar continued to suffer these regular assaults in silence. The attacks left physical and emotional scars on both of them. Magdalena later said she learned not to resist because that was always more painful emotionally and physically. She also started to believe that it was all her fault that she was being assaulted to such an extent that in the end she just presumed what was happening to her was normal.

It was only when Magdalena and Eleazar reached their early teens that they began to realise that they needed to escape their evil relatives. The final straw came when Magdalena thought she'd been made pregnant by her own father, only to discover it had been a false alarm. Both she and her brother Eleazar knew that if she'd turned out to be pregnant she would have been trapped in the village for the rest of her life. That was when the pair decided it was time to escape.

In the middle of a scorching hot summer's night in 1960, Magdalena and Eleazar each packed themselves a small bag of clothes and tiptoed out of the back of the run-down wooden shack the family called home.

The pair headed for the nearest big city of Monterrey, where they'd heard there were plentiful jobs and people could afford such luxuries as television sets and cars. But the streets of Monterrey in the early 1960s turned out to be a brutal place for two teenagers who could barely read or write. Without a permanent address, the pair couldn't even get themselves a menial job, let alone a place to sleep.

Naive and desperate, Magdalena and Eleazar began begging on the streets to survive. They quickly discovered that the homeless people of Monterrey fiercely guarded anything they considered their 'territory'. Eleazar was badly beaten by a gang of drifters and Magdalena only just escaped being raped by two homeless men in an attack that brought back all the painful memories of her childhood, as well as further convincing her that everything happening to her was her fault.

So when a kind-looking, middle-aged woman offered them a bed to stay, the pair never questioned her motivations. It was only the following morning over breakfast that the woman told them Magdalena would have to work as a prostitute to pay off the rent for the pair having stayed with her. The woman was the owner of a local brothel.

At the age of just 13, Magdalena found herself having to sleep with men for money. It was at least, she later declared, far preferable to being raped by her father. She even tried to block out those memories of what he'd done to her throughout her childhood but it wasn't easy.

Magdalena also persuaded the brothel madam to allow Eleazar to stay with her in her room after he reluctantly agreed to sleep with any gay clients who required his services. However, Magdalena knew that Eleazar was a much more sensitive soul than her, so she went out of her way to go with as many male clients as possible in the hope his services would not be required very often.

Eleazar eventually became his sister's personal pimp, protecting her from physical attacks by any male clients and also making sure they actually paid the money to sleep with her. It was cold, mindless and very disturbing work but they had little choice in the matter. All these experiences only served to further convince Magdalena that all men were evil, except for her beloved baby brother of course. And she eventually managed to cut off emotionally from the disturbing reality of having sex with anonymous men.

Inside the brothel where Magdalena worked, other women constantly accused her of being rude to the male customers. The brothel madam even began ordering her to smile more, saying her constant frown was bad for business.

Magdalena gradually found a niche inside the brothel because a surprisingly large number of the men wanted to be humiliated by her. She would curse and beat them, at their own orders. When some of them dared to complain that she'd beaten them up too violently, she'd just shrug her shoulders and tell them where to go and Eleazar would frequently have to then step in to stop them attacking her.

Magdalena later confessed that hurting those men was good for her head, as she was able to exorcise many of the demons she'd had since those childhood attacks by her father. But when one of the other women working in the brothel encouraged the girl to join her church, Magdalena began to feel like she should clean up her life.

She'd spent most of her childhood hating the Church, feeling it had 'allowed' her father and others to abuse her. Now, however, it was giving her an emotional outlet she never thought existed.

When Eleazar dismissed her new-found religious beliefs, she told him God would forgive her for working as a prostitute and he should start going to church with her, in search of the same forgiveness.

Magdalena went to confession to further cleanse her soul. In the confessional box, she admitted what she did for a job to the priest who ran the church. He admonished her for her sins, even as she begged forgiveness. Afterwards the priest began treating her with disgust. During Sunday services, Magdalena began noticing the priest looking down at her with contempt while she was accepting sacramental bread from him.

One weekday morning, Magdalena was in church on her knees praying when the priest appeared next to her and ordered her to visit his vestry behind the altar. After entering, Magdalena stood in an awkward silence waiting for the priest to say something. He eventually ordered her to take her clothes off, saying it was time for her to finally be rid of her sins.

Magdalena knew immediately that what he was saying was wrong, but she was afraid of upsetting God, so she did what he said. But to her it was even worse than the way men had treated her throughout her life because he was supposed to be a man of the Church.

From that moment on, she hated that priest as much as she had loathed her father. Worse still, she was convinced no one would believe her if she tried to tell them what had happened. To the community, he was a saintly priest and she was nothing more than a 'common whore'.

When Magdalena broke down and told her brother Eleazar what had happened, he was angry and told her he was going to burn the church down. But Magdalena stopped him. She told him she'd decided that what had happened was a message from the Devil telling her she could work in the brothel after all. This, tragically, marked the beginning of the end of Magdalena's interest in so-called 'normal' religion.

She'd always been told as a child that she and her brother were possessed by the Devil and this had made those attacks on them feel almost legitimate. Now – despite all the terrible things done to her in the name of black magic – she believed the Devil was turning out to be a better friend to her than Jesus Christ.

Magdalena's revived interest in the occult brought her into contact with a black magic priest and priestess in Monterrey. The pair were magnetic, manipulative characters and Magdalena soon fell under their spell.

She also started reading tarot cards to housewives during afternoon sessions before the brothel opened for business. She slept with both men and women she met through those occult activities, but she gradually realised it was the women who most ignited her passion.

For the first time in her life, Magdalena began to experience loving, sexual relations without money being involved, and to enjoy it. On some afternoons off from the brothel, she began visiting gay bars and picking up women.

She still needed to work in the brothel to afford to live, but by this time most of the men only expected her to beat them up, so she was spared having to have sex with them. Magdalena also convinced herself that being a dominatrix was completely in keeping with her revived interest in the occult.

She began opening up about her disturbing childhood to some of her gay lovers and even told them about how she'd had sex with her father. Magdalena also implied to these people that she'd forced children to sleep with her. They thought she was fantasising because they had no idea that her own brutal childhood experiences had turned her into a perpetrator after spending so much time as the victim.

The traumatic attacks she'd suffered had eaten into Magdalena's psyche. She believed she had the right to abuse children in the way she had been abused. It was a twisted form of payback which had turned Magdalena into a dark force.

* * *

One hundred miles from Monterrey lay the tiny, sleepy hamlet of Yerba Buena. Hidden deep among the dusty drylands of the high sierra, it didn't even classify as a village, it was so small. In Spanish it was referred to as an *ejido*, or communal farm, comprising just 20 families. There were no schools, police or even a church in Yerba Buena. The poor, mostly illiterate population survived on subsistence farming, selling corn and beans from their fields in the nearby towns.

Then one day in 1962, two grifter brothers called Santos and Cayetano Hernández rode into Yerba Buena on horseback, having just been run out of a town 50 miles to the east. The pair rarely stayed anywhere for long once the locals had worked out what they were up to and they'd survived for years dreaming up new money-making schemes, which relied on the naivety of the residents of isolated places just like Yerba Buena.

The Hernández brothers informed all the locals that they were prophets of the ancient Incan gods. Using classic, sleight-of-hand card tricks, they also convinced the tiny community that they had supernatural powers.

The irony of all this was that if the inhabitants of Yerba Buena had had proper access to Mexican ancient history books, they'd have known that the brothers' claims were nonsense because the Incas came from Peru, not Mexico. The brothers should have told the locals they were there on behalf of the Aztec gods, as they actually did come from Mexico.

This pair of tricksters promised the locals that if they joined their movement, they'd end up with vast riches thanks to the legendary treasure they claimed was hidden in the caves high up in the surrounding eastern Sierra Madre mountains. But the brothers also warned the locals that the gods would punish any non-believers. They began holding intricate rituals fuelled by cannabis-laced incense in Yerba Buena. The brothers performed animal sacrifices inside one of the biggest caves overlooking Yerba Buena to try and 'persuade the gods to reveal where the treasure was hidden'.

Once they had a village's trust, the brothers would announce to all the residents that they would have to make a cash donation to them. When some citizens of Yerba Buena claimed they had no money, the brothers suggested those residents with no money should be trained to work as their slaves in exchange for allowing them to attend their services. The two were even given a house to live in free of charge, as well as round-the-clock food and drink provided by their 'servants'.

The Hernández brothers then announced to the residents of Yerba Buena that the next round of ritual ceremonies held in the caves required all teenage girls to attend, along with their families. They insisted that the girls should be given to them as a gift and that they would teach them how to get in touch with the gods, who'd provide the community with all that treasure. Even when the brothers said that the teenage girls would not be returned to their families, no one dared object.

The brothers sold the girls off to sex traffickers, who dispatched them to the border towns where they were forced to work in brothels or out on the streets. They then convinced the locals that their daughters had gone off to work in proper, legitimate jobs and would be back soon with lots of money for them.

The Hernández brothers then began demanding sex from all the remaining women in Yerba Buena, with their supposed rituals evolving into sex orgies. The two proclaimed themselves to be prophets and high priests of those 'powerful and exiled Incan gods' who would help them all find those great riches, and if anyone dared question their authority, the two brothers would immediately threaten to punish them for 'non believing'.

And as their confidence increased, so their demands became more outrageous. The brothers introduced economic and sexual 'taxes' for both male and female residents, and ordered many of the locals to ingest hallucinogenic drugs as part of their rituals. This would enable them to hold even more explicit sex orgies, which they still claimed would help uncover all that treasure hidden in the surrounding caves. But when the promised riches still hadn't materialised after almost six months, some of the residents began wondering if the brothers' psychic powers were really genuine.

Recognising that there could be problems on the horizon, the brothers announced to their flock of followers that they'd just been summoned to the highest mountain tops by the gods to meet a new goddess, who would have the power to guarantee that the treasures in the caves would finally be uncovered. They then headed straight to Monterrey, the largest nearby city and home to many of the sex traffickers they'd previously sold Yerba Buena's teenage girls to.

Within hours of arriving in the city, the brothers headed to the brothel where Magdalena Solís was working. Both of them had paid for her services during a previous visit to Monterrey and she'd told them about her black magic interests and tarot card reading skills. She perfectly fitted the bill to be their goddess, and the brothers began to concoct a plan.

Magdalena had just started another new sideline as a fortune-teller and medium. She claimed she could channel the spirits of long-dead *brujas* (priests of the occult) during séances she held, mainly with housewives, on afternoons when she was not working in the brothel.

When the Hernández brothers told Magdalena about their black magic scam in Yerba Buena, she saw it as an opportunity to earn a fortune from an already tame audience prepared to connect with occultist beliefs. Delighted by the opportunity, she quit the brothel in Monterrey.

However, Magdalena wanted her brother Eleazar to join them in Yerba Buena, and insisted to the brothers that he be allowed. They weren't keen but agreed to Magdalena's demands, as they knew she'd make the perfect goddess and was integral to the plan.

The following day, the Hernández brothers returned to Yerba Buena. They asked their goddess Magdalena and her brother to hide in woodland outside the village to give them time to talk everything through with their disciples.

In Yerba Buena, the brothers sat the locals down and carefully explained that the goddess would soon be joining them. But first they all had to make a cash contribution to their church to ensure her safe arrival. This time every member of the community paid up.

Later that evening, the entire population of the village gathered in their small community square in anticipation of the goddess's arrival. The brothers ordered the villagers to wait in complete silence as they burned stacks of firewood which spread thick, atmospheric clouds of smoke across the plaza.

Goddess Magdalena Solís appeared dressed in a black cloak with thick make-up looking like an apparition. Many residents were so dumbstruck, they immediately knelt in front of the goddess, who began personally anointing each one of them on the shoulder with a sword.

Magdalena later admitted that she adored the feeling of power invested in her by the community that night. For the first time in her life, she felt wanted and special.

That evening, Magdalena and brother Eleazar stayed in the Hernández's detached home on the outskirts of Yerba Buena.

At first, all four of them got on well but the brother and sister sensed the atmosphere becoming darker as the Hernández pair consumed copious amounts of alcohol and drugs.

Noticing this, Magdalena made her excuses and went to bed. But after she left, the brothers became very suggestive towards Eleazar. Initially, he laughed off their comments but then they made it clear they wanted to sleep with him. He later said he felt obliged to do it to help protect his sister and find out what their true intentions were. The brothers had big plans to use the pair to entice even more villagers to join their cult.

The following morning, Eleazar reported to Magdalena about this and how the brothers were going to order the citizens to visit the sacred, surrounding caves and redecorate their interiors, so that they were good enough for the goddess to pray in. Magdalena liked the sound of this and even brushed off her brother's complaints about the way they'd treated him.

Once the caves had been refurbished, they were used for sex orgies with men and women as newly arrived Goddess Magdalena looked on hungrily while ordering them to perform in front of her. She found it easy to convince the disciples that having sex would please the Devil so much that the treasures inside these very same caves would soon belong to them all.

Huge quantities of hallucinogenic drugs were administered to the locals at these ceremonies, which made them even more susceptible to Goddess Magdalena's twisted whims and desires. In addition to numerous sex acts, she ordered the locals to perform animal sacrifices and then drink the creature's blood, which she insisted would help them all gain immortality.

Within days, Goddess Magdalena's demands had escalated further, as she ordered the villagers to have sex with live animals which would then be killed. This was followed by enforced incest between family members in front of a live audience of disciples. The goddess continued insisting such twisted practices would help cleanse them.

The community of Yerba Buena was so in awe of the goddess by this time that they provided her with the largest house in the community to live in. She seemed to be already overtaking the Hernández brothers in terms of influence.

Magdalena adored the way that the disciples unquestionably did exactly what she demanded, even down to sleeping with each other whenever she ordered it. At mealtimes, Magdalena didn't need to lift a finger because the women of the community cooked all her food and brought it to her in the house and then did everything else she demanded.

Goddess Magdalena often granted these women permission to stay with her on condition they slept with her after she'd finished eating. However, the presence of the goddess still hadn't led to the discovery of the infamous treasure promised by the Hernández brothers, and two of the male disciples started questioning the authenticity of it all.

When Goddess Magdalena heard about the two dissenters, she accused them of being 'unbelievers' and insisted the two men were disciples of Satan sent to Yerba Buena to upset the community and prevent them getting their hands on the treasure. Within days, both men had been killed by their own frightened neighbours. The Hernández brothers were impressed by the way Magdalena had dealt with the men, even though it would inevitably give her more power and influence within the community.

Over the following six weeks, half a dozen more alleged dissenters were beaten to death during ritual ceremonies hosted in the caves by Goddess Magdalena and the two Hernández brothers. Under strict orders from Magdalena, disciples beat, burned and hacked at their victims with machetes until they died. Magdalena began to insist the victims' blood was blended with chicken blood in sacrificial goblets before being drunk by everyone present in the caves following each ritual killing.

It was gradually dawning on the Hernández brothers that they'd helped create their own monster in Goddess Magdalena. She had the disciples that once 'belonged' to them eating out of her hand. They'd watched all this happening with admiration at first but now they were starting to wonder if it was time to rein her in.

Meanwhile Magdalena and her brother Eleazar were being supplied with so much cannabis and peyote by her disciples that they'd developed a round-the-clock drug habit. The narcotics even convinced Magdalena that she really was a goddess and she started telling her disciples she was the secret reincarnation of the Aztec mother goddess called Coatlicue. At least this mythical figure was actually Mexican, which made her claims a lot more believable than the Hernández brothers' previous fabrications.

Any villagers openly questioning these claims would find themselves dragged on to a makeshift altar where they'd be beaten to a pulp and often killed. Goddess Magdalena began replicating ancient Aztec sacrificial rituals by making disciples cut the hearts out of some victims, often while they were still alive.

As one Yerba Buena resident later explained: 'She seemed so credible to most of us. We believed in the Devil and so when she presented herself as a goddess to us and ordered us to do certain things, we just accepted that she had to be right. She made it seem as if we were at war with the rest of the world and the only way to win that war was to do exactly what she said.'

While Magdalena believed she was ultimately in control of everything happening in Yerba Buena, the older Hernández brother Cayetano was diverted by some problems on the other side of the *ejido*. One of the disciples believed he'd worked out the brothers' scam and he wanted a piece of their 'pie' in exchange for not blowing the lid on them. Cayetano Hernández was so outraged to be shaken down by one of Yerba Buena's residents that he refused to pay the man, who then promptly shot him dead.

Back at the ranch's main altar, Magdalena was informed that Cayetano had gone missing but no one realised he was actually dead. So she continued to demand sex with anyone who took her fancy at all times of the day or night.

Two men she forced to sleep with her that day had been so traumatised by their experiences that they'd begun to look more closely at her credentials to be an occult goddess. When one of them found Magdalena sobbing in a toilet at her house shortly after they'd all slept together, the men became even more convinced she was not the goddess she'd made out she was to them. Magdalena was still in two minds about what to do next about Cayetano's disappearance. In some ways it was good news because she could further consolidate her power base, but it also meant that if disaffected locals were involved in snatching him then maybe she'd be next on their 'hit list'.

A few days later, the same two men who'd started looking more closely at Magdalena's credentials stood up in the audience during yet another sex ritual in the caves and began questioning her closely about her background.

Later that same evening, three of Magdalena's most loyal disciples and her brother Eleazar informed her that they'd been told the same two men planned to run away from the sect and go to the authorities. Magdalena ordered Eleazar and her followers to bring the two would-be defectors to her immediately.

After being dragged through the backyard of her spacious detached house, Magdalena ordered the men to kneel in front of her and promptly sentenced them to death. Then she turned to her other disciples and ordered them to carry out the killing on her behalf.

The two men were dragged away and lynched by half a dozen locals. Many of the 50-plus members of the original community were in such a frenzied state by this time that they didn't even know why they were killing in the first place.

Magdalena saw this all as a clear sign that she still had complete and utter control over the entire community and all its residents. Surviving Hernández brother Santos had become more marginalised since his brother's mysterious disappearance.

Shortly after the murder of the two 'unbelievers', Magdalena, drunk on her power, ordered families to bring her their children. When she was alone with the children, she sexually molested them before beating them up so they would never dare tell anyone else what had happened to them.

Goddess Magdalena then devised a new type of ritual during which followers were brutally beaten, burned, cut and maimed by other disciples while Magdalena sat spread-legged on her makeshift throne openly masturbating as she watched it all.

After noisily climaxing, Magdalena insisted on watching some victims bleed to death. She assured her disciples that these rituals gave them all unique, supernatural powers that would ensure everlasting invincibility.

She told them: 'This blood is the only food the gods want and it guarantees the preservation of your immortality.'

By this time, Magdalena only ever referred to herself as 'The High Priestess of Blood' and smeared herself in blood to further enhance her own sexual excitement, as well as convincing the audience of her own immortality.

She announced to her disciples that she would only have sex when she was in the middle of her menstrual cycle. She began cutting herself deliberately and then emptying her own blood into cups, which she then drank in front of her disciples while climaxing. And her loyal younger brother Eleazar remained at her side much of the time. He later said he tried to stop her stepping completely over the line. But whatever the truth of the matter, he had little real influence over his sister by this time.

On one evening in May 1963, a 14-year-old local youth, Sebastian Guerrero, was out walking in the hills behind Yerba Buena when he noticed flickering lights coming from inside one of the caves that had been regularly used for rituals. As he crept quietly through the darkness, Guerrero heard the sounds of people screaming and wailing. He could also smell incense and recognised it as probably being copal, a special resin first invented by the Aztecs, which he'd heard was used during rituals.

The teenager edged slowly towards the mouth of the cave, careful to stay out of sight. When he was close enough, he cautiously peered inside and witnessed an appalling scene.

More than a dozen Yerba Buena residents were assembled inside the candlelit cave. Some were naked and openly engaging in sex on the floor next to the altar. Others were passing around a ceremonial chalice and drinking dark red fluid from it.

On the other side of the same elaborate altar, Guerrero noticed a disciple leaning over the hacked-up remains of a corpse draining blood out of the stomach area. And standing above this disciple was Goddess Magdalena, holding up the bleeding heart of the same man whose body lay crumpled on the stone floor in front of her.

The teenager was so petrified by what he saw that he immediately turned and ran down the steep mountainside. He didn't stop running for more than three hours, until he reached the nearest police station in the farming town of Villa Gran, 25 kilometres from Yerba Buena.

Exhausted and still in shock, the teenager could barely speak as he tried to explain to a duty officer what he'd seen earlier that evening. In the end, he just managed to blurt out that there had been 'a group of murderers who prey on ecstasy and who were gluttonously drinking human blood like vampires'.

The officer laughed at the youth's dramatic statement and then accused him of taking drugs himself. When the teenager insisted he was telling the truth and mentioned that the cult leader was a woman, the officer laughed even louder.

Listening to all this from a nearby desk was police detective Luis Martínez. He had relatives who lived near Yerba Buena and had heard rumours of a cult operating there. Martínez got up and insisted on interviewing the teenager himself.

Within half an hour, Martínez was convinced the youngster's story was genuine. Early the following morning, he escorted the teenager back to the Yerba Buena area.

The schoolboy initially took Martínez to where he'd seen the 'vampires' in the cave the previous night. After examining multiple bloodstains in the main cave, detective Martínez and the youngster walked down the hillside to be greeted by Magdalena and Santos Hernández.

The cult leaders had received reports earlier from some of their disciples of Yerba Buena that the boy and the policeman had been seen heading for the caves. Sebastian Guerrero and Luis Martínez were never again seen alive.

When neither of them returned to the police station back in Villa Gran, other investigators decided to take immediate action. On 31 May 1963, police – in conjunction with the Mexican army – assembled a task force to raid Yerba Buena.

Within hours, multiple units were swarming through the valley but the residents had already been warned that the police were most likely on their way and had abandoned their properties earlier that morning. As the police and army surveyed the empty community, the eerie silence that had enveloped the valley was suddenly broken by gunshots being fired at them from the caves above.

A shoot-out lasting more than two hours followed. Only a dozen disciples survived. They were rounded up and hand-cuffed before being taken in police vehicles to the nearest jail.

On the outskirts of Yerba Buena, law enforcement discovered Magdalena and her brother Eleazar hiding in a farmhouse high on drugs and boxes packed with cannabis were stacked up in the hallway. Magdalena and Eleazar were immediately arrested but Santos Hernández emerged from a small hut and made a run for it through the land behind the property. He was shot dead by police as he tried to climb over a wall, having refused an order to surrender.

The remains of teenager Sebastian Guerrero and police officer Luis Martínez were found close to the main farmhouse. Martínez's heart had been removed in the style of the Aztec sacrifice that Magdalena had encouraged her disciples to take part in.

On the other side of the Yerba Buena compound, the body of Cayetano Hernández was found. The remains of six more dismembered bodies were eventually discovered by investigators close to the same caves, where many of the black magic rituals had been held.

A total of 14 Yerba Buena disciples were eventually arrested and sentenced to 30 years in prison after being directly linked to the murder of at least six other residents. In court, the killings were described as 'group or gang murder, or lynching'.

Defence attorneys cited the disciples' poverty and lack of education as mitigating circumstances as to why they were so easily lured into becoming such avid followers of the Hernández's sick and twisted black magic movement.

Magdalena and her brother Eleazar later stood trial in Ciudad Victoria but no Yerba Buena residents would testify against them. In the end, Magdalena and Eleazar were only convicted of the murders of schoolboy Sebastian Guerrero and police detective Martínez. The brother and sister were eventually sentenced to 50 years each. All those present at the trial noted how little Eleazar said in his own defence, and it soon became clear, he was entirely under the control of his older sister.

After Magdalena's sentencing, authorities alleged that she'd been involved in as many as 15 other murders, many of which were claimed to have occurred after victims refused to have sex with her. These revelations meant Magdalena was one of only a tiny number of female serial killers whose murders had been sexually motivated. However, many criminologists have since pointed out that she and her brother were undoubtedly seeking revenge for what happened during her own childhood, although none of that warranted their murderous actions.

What happened to Magdalena after she was sent to prison remains a mystery to this day. It has been strongly rumoured that she died in prison and was given a pauper's funeral in order to stop her grave site becoming an altar to her dark occultist activities. The fate of her brother Eleazar is equally mysterious. He was sent to one of Mexico's most notorious prisons and has never been heard of since.

The families of some of Magdalena's victims remain convinced to this day she will eventually be released from prison and given a new identity to prevent them from seeking revenge on her for the deaths of their loved ones. But like so much of Magdalena's life, it's impossible to be certain of anything except the horror she inflicted on so many innocent people.

CHAPTER THREE

THE SISTERS OF THE INFERNO
DELFINA AND MARÍA TORRES

In the sleepy town of El Salto de Juanacatlán, Jalisco, neighbours of the Torres family had grown used to a lot of screaming and shouting coming from their home. Despite this, no one confronted the so-called man of the house Isidro Torres, as he was a notoriously volatile local police officer.

Even when Torres dragged his two young daughters Delfina and María out of the front door and down the wooden steps to the front yard furiously yelling at them, the other residents in their street stayed quiet. Some of them watched from their front windows, though, as Torres left his daughters crying in the dust and marched over to his truck and got in. He fired up the rattling V-8 and reversed it to where they lay sobbing.

With the engine still running, Torres flung open the driver's door and stomped round to the back of the truck to flip down the tailgate. He stood over his two daughters for a few moments staring at them with contempt. Then he leaned down, pulled them roughly to their feet and dragged them by their hair on to the wooden flat bed in the back of the truck.

Ordering them both not to move, he noisily flung the tailgate shut before walking back and getting in the driver's seat and slamming the door. Crunching the truck into gear, he screeched off in a cloud of dust. Five minutes later, Torres pulled into a car park behind a darkened building. He flipped down the back of the truck, dragged his daughters out and marched them towards a back door marked 'Solo Policía' (Police Only).

Inside the police station, the duty officer rolled his eyes and looked the other way as Torres passed him with his two daughters. He yanked them down some steps to a corridor underneath the building, which contained six barred cells.

Torres stopped at one of the cells, pushed it open and then shoved his two children in, locking the door behind them. He put his face close to the bars and told them he never wanted to see them wearing make-up ever again or he'd tell the town's most feared sexual predator to rape them so that no man would ever go near them again. The two girls didn't dare cry in case their father came into the cell and beat them again, but once they were certain he'd gone, they sobbed their hearts out.

That night, the two young girls barely slept. The male inmates in the other cells kept shouting obscenities at them and one elderly man even masturbated through the bars of the cell opposite, laughing as he did it. Delfina and María later recalled the night in the police station cell as something that would haunt them for the rest of their lives.

Early the following morning, Torres appeared outside their cell and made both his daughters repeat after him that they would never again wear make-up without his permission. They were just 11 and 12 years old and had just been trying on the make-up out of curiosity while their mother was out shopping with their four younger brothers and sisters. In 1930s Mexico, though, such behaviour was seen as defiant, rebellious and immoral.

That night, Torres told his wife and daughters over supper that he only punished them for their own protection and demanded that all the women in his household must only wear black dresses, shawls and head scarves. Later both girls realised it all boiled down to him being a misogynistic bully. He continually made it abundantly clear that women were there to serve him and nothing else.

Isidro Torres's harsh and senseless brutality towards his family was an extension of his abusive and authoritarian attitude that he took on patrol with him. On the pretext that he wanted to ensure the streets were safe, he would patrol El Salto de Juanacatlán, brutally punishing anyone he saw breaking his rules.

During one public holiday called Día de la Revolución – which commemorated Mexico's independence – Torres got in an argument with a local man in a bar and shot him dead.

He wasn't even reprimanded by his superiors, though, as he insisted that the other man had threatened him first.

Torres's ongoing reign of terror in El Salto de Juanacatlán was also dangerous for Delfina and María and the rest of their family, as there were a growing number of men in the town who loathed the policeman and wanted him gone for ever. The family began receiving anonymous death threats. Twice, Torres was ambushed by gunmen after being called out to attend fake crimes that were reported in order to lure him to his death.

In the end, even Torres's state police bosses decided that his reign of terror needed to come to an end sooner rather than later. Torres was given no option but to quit his job as a policeman, otherwise, said his bosses, they would be forced to officially fire him.

So – just a few months after shooting dead that man in the bar – Torres, his long-suffering wife Bernardina Valenzuela and their six children, including daughters Delfina and María, relocated 50 miles east to the small village of San Francisco del Rincón, Guanajuato. It was known as San Pancho to most locals who lived there.

Torres's physical intimidation and abuse of his two older daughters continued, even though the family were now living in an isolated community which had virtually no other children of their age. He was drinking so much that often he couldn't even remember what he'd done to his daughters by the following day. And Delfina and María's mother and other younger brothers and sisters never once tried to stop Torres attacking them because they were all terrified of him. As the sisters' fear of their father turned to sheer hatred and hardened within them, they became increasingly convinced that all men were out to hurt them, just like he'd done over and over again.

When Torres came home one evening from his new job in a nearby stone quarry, he exploded yet again after noticing that both Delfina and María were wearing party dresses and had make-up on their faces. He immediately accused his daughters of going out with boys. This time they defiantly glared back at their father, which he immediately presumed was further proof they were what he called 'whores'.

Torres dragged both of them by their hair out into the dusty yard behind their home, where he slapped them around before forcing them on their knees to crawl into the tiny entrance of a run-down dog kennel, which he then blocked with a big stone. The two children were left in that flimsy wooden hut for 24 hours without food and water. Each time their mother tried to persuade Torres to let her see her two daughters, he slapped his wife across the face until she cried.

Delfina and María were only released by their father after they'd meekly agreed never to wear make-up again. Then they scurried off to the bedroom they shared with their other brothers and sisters to avoid any further beatings.

Delfina and María shared many intimate secrets with each other during their troubled childhood. But the most blinding one of all was their continued hatred and contempt for their father.

Neither Delfina nor María were allowed to leave the family home for months following that latest incident with their father. Torres even banned them from attending school after accusing them of having sex with men while they were out of the house. This deeply impacted the two sisters and they became convinced they had to plan a future for themselves away from their father and the rest of their traumatised family.

Having discussed it at great length, they concluded that the only way to make enough money to escape was to do the very thing their drunken bully of a father had accused them of over and over again. So both sisters – now in their mid-teens – persuaded their mother to allow them to sleep with men for money at the family house while Torres was at work and their other siblings were at school. They believed that Torres would never find out because the men who paid them would be too ashamed to tell anyone they had slept with the two sisters.

For almost two years, Delfina and María sold their bodies to men for money behind the back of their father, who believed he'd stopped them misbehaving by not allowing them out of the house while he was at work. However, it was a harrowing existence for the two teenagers. Both sisters were regularly attacked and raped by customers. A lot of men didn't pay them for sex after threatening them with guns. The sisters also had to pay a cut of their earnings to their own mother, who had threatened to tell their father if they didn't.

Delfina and María later recalled there were many occasions when they wanted to quit, but the alternative was an entire life under their father's brutal regime. It wasn't until the two sisters had reached their late teens that they'd saved up enough cash to finally escape their village, and they chose a night when their father was passed out drunk on the front porch of the family home.

With everything they owned packed into two small suitcases, Delfina and María slipped out of the back of the house and didn't tell their mother or siblings for fear they would tell Torres. The sisters caught a bus to the bustling mining town of Lagos, Jalisco, and sank their savings into a bar, which they bought from a gay man known dismissively by locals as 'El Poquianchi', which referred in slang to the small size of his penis.

New owners Delfina and María became known as Las Poquianchis (the small dicks), which they hated because it linked them to the previous owner and implied they were pathetic, masculine women. But the bar struggled to attract enough business because most local men preferred to drink in brothels, which were filled with women they could sleep with.

Delfina and María abandoned all their aspirations of running a genuine bar and converted their premises into a bordello, promising alcohol and sex and all other desires, which they called 'Inferno'. It was an apt name because locals soon proclaimed it was a den of vice inspired by the Devil. Inferno earned a reputation for having the most attractive women in the area. Delfina and María proudly boasted that was all down to them.

Within six months, the sisters had made so much money that they opened a second brothel in a nearby town. Delfina and María's younger sisters, Carmen and María Luisa, then joined their business and ran other new premises in Guanajuato and Jalisco. The sisters also bought another brothel close to the Mexican border.

Despite the booming business, the sisters found it increasingly hard to find women to work in their brothels. They scoured the countryside in Guanajuato plus rural Jalisco and Michoacán states on recruitment drives.

By this time, Delfina was in a relationship with former Mexican army officer Hermenegildo Zuniga, known by the nickname 'The Black Eagle'. The couple had two children together and were as good as married.

Delfina and her lover eventually started kidnapping women from deserted country lanes and forcing them to work in the brothels. The terrified women were warned that if they didn't co-operate, then their families would be killed.

Delfina and María would trap a lot of these women into staying in their brothels by getting them hooked on heroin and cocaine. Once they were addicted, it was then even harder for the women to escape.

Many had only fallen into drug addiction as a means of escaping the reality of their appalling predicaments. But they became like putty in the hands of the sisters and those who ran each brothel.

The administrative staff at each location consisted of mainly misogynistic henchmen. They were often ordered to guard the youngest and most innocent girls, so they could be offered to the richest patrons.

Many of the women working in the sisters' brothels were raped by the male staff members, who believed they had a right to have sex for free with them. The women were also forced to buy all their clothes and make-up only from the sisters, who charged them higher than usual prices. In addition to taking a 50 per cent cut from every sexual transaction, Delfina and María earned even more money by selling alcohol and drugs at inflated prices inside their brothels.

Delfina's oldest son, Ramon 'El Tepo' Torres, worked as a bodyguard and front-door bouncer at one brothel from the age of 17. The teenager kept many of the sex workers in line, so they didn't misbehave or upset the customers.

Delfina and María had some rich and powerful customers at their brothels including judges, law enforcement officers, military personnel and even politicians. Some were even paying the sisters 'premium prices' to sleep with young virgins kept locked up until they were required. Other regular customers also included soldiers, councilmen, police officers and even male residents from the villages and towns where the brothels were located.

One teenage sex worker later alleged that the sisters had an abortionist on the payroll who would 'take care' of any of the girls who got pregnant. 'They were given no choice in the matter and often beaten up for getting pregnant in the first place,' the woman recalled.

These abortions were usually carried out in a back room at the bordellos and bloody foetuses would be dumped in dustbins in the backyard of each property. A number of foetuses were also buried in the ground next to the sisters' newly acquired ranch called Loma del Angel, located next door to one of their most successful brothels.

Witnesses later described the conditions inside the sisters' brothels as being akin to concentration camps, with women living and working in tiny, crumbling bedrooms, often no bigger than a jail cell. Many women became sick through malnourishment or STDs. Others suffered haemorrhaging following botched abortions. These women would simply be locked in their rooms until they'd recovered.

Some women later alleged that they were sometimes forced by the sisters' male henchmen to beat already seriously ill women to death with sticks and heavy logs, so that their rooms could be vacated for other sex workers to use.

Delfina, her lover (Hermenegildo 'The Black Eagle' Zuniga) and their young male chauffeur would apparently often stand and watch while these human 'culls' were carried out. Male henchmen would then either burn the corpses or bury them in a mass grave next to the sisters' ranch.

* * *

Over the years, the sisters also got increasingly greedy. Richer customers at the brothels would be forced to hand over all their cash at gunpoint and would be murdered by the brothel henchmen if they refused to co-operate.

In the summer of 1963, Delfina's trigger-happy son 'El Tepo' got into a shouting match with two local policemen in the bar of one of the sisters' brothels and ended up being shot dead by the officers.

The police immediately raided the premises and closed it down. Delfina was so devastated by the death of her son that she ordered Zuniga to track down the officers who did it and kill them, which he duly did. Zuniga was never arrested following the murder of the two cops and there were strong rumours that Delfina paid off corrupt police officers and other officials to drop the investigation.

Delfina, María and their other siblings were by this stage so immersed in the tainted world of vice and drugs that they didn't once realise they'd actually morphed into deadlier versions of their own hated father.

By the end of 1963, Delfina and María's sex businesses was so successful that they believed they were virtually untouchable, thanks to their VIP clientele's powerful connections. Then in early January 1964, a woman called Catalina Ortega – who worked in the sisters' brothel next to their Loma del Angel ranch – squeezed through a small window in the wall of her bedroom and went on the run.

Delfina only found out what had happened when one of the other women working in the brothel informed her because she was scared she'd be blamed for not stopping the other girl from leaving. Delfina knew it was imperative to capture Catalina before she spoke to anyone, so she sent Zuniga out to search for and then eliminate Catalina. Zuniga and his henchmen combed the area for more than 24 hours without finding any trace of her.

The girl had actually managed to travel through the night to reach her mother's home in the neighbouring city of León. The two women immediately went to the city's Judicial Police. Catalina told them all about the sisters and their murderous habits.

But the two officers who initially spoke to Catalina and her mother refused to believe their allegations. Catalina later said she thought she recognised one of the policemen from when he'd visited the brothel a few weeks earlier.

Catalina and her mother were about to give up and leave the police station when another younger officer took pity on them. He encouraged Catalina to provide a full statement about what had happened to her.

Armed with this evidence, the police got an official search warrant issued by a judge at short notice. On 14 January 1964, they headed in a convoy of vehicles to the brothel next to the Loma del Angel ranch from where Catalina had earlier escaped.

As law enforcement officers accompanied by journalists swarmed through the ranch, they came across more than a dozen dirty and malnourished women huddled in two run-down rooms at the back of the main farmhouse. At the front, a door flew open to reveal two women dressed entirely in black and wearing shawls staring defiantly at the police. It was María and Delfina, still mourning the death of Delfina's son El Tepo months after he'd died.

They were immediately identified by some of the bedraggled sex workers and handcuffed by officers. Their prisoners pointed out to the authorities specific locations in the grounds where the sisters had buried men, women and even unborn children as María and Delfina sneered at them all. The sex workers also referred to satanic rites and how some girls had been forced to have sex with animals as well as multiple men during bizarre sacrificial ceremonies inside the main ranch house.

Watching all this still in handcuffs from the front of the main farmhouse, the sisters showed no emotion whatsoever. When one police officer asked Delfina how the bodies got there, she reportedly replied: 'The food didn't sit well with them.'

Meanwhile Delfina's driver was ordered by police to begin digging up the area where the victims were alleged to have been buried. He did this until police officers arrived at the scene with mechanical diggers and took over the search. The remains of at least 100 corpses would eventually be uncovered.

As word of the case spread, an angry mob of villagers began to gather outside the ranch demanding that the sisters be lynched. When Delfina and María were escorted to a waiting police cruiser, they screamed back obscenities at the furious crowd of onlookers.

Later that same day, both sisters were charged with multiple homicides at a nearby police station. They were then ordered to be taken in a prison van under heavy military guard to a maximum security jail in nearby San Francisco del Rincón.

Midway through the cross-country journey, though, the convoy was diverted to a smaller, more run-down prison at Irapuato, which was considered 'safer and more escape-proof'. The police had been tipped off that the sisters had so many friends in high places they might be sprung from the bigger prison.

A week later, Delfina and María's sister María Luisa González known as 'Eva the Leggy One' walked into a Mexico City police station and turned herself in, fearing that she'd be attacked when the locals living near the brothel she ran found out who she was.

María Luisa believed she'd be immune from any actual criminal charges because of her connections to several local judges, who regularly used the brothel she ran. But María Luisa was immediately arrested and taken away to be interviewed.

As news of the raids reached the media, dozens of sex workers came forward to openly accuse the sisters of rape, murder and extortion. Delfina, María and María Luisa's eventual trial in 1964 was chaotic, as the defiant sisters would openly threaten women giving evidence against them. Delfina and María were eventually sentenced to 40 years each in prison for killing a total of 91 people.

Delfina suffered psychotic episodes inside prison within months of being sentenced. Psychiatrists later suggested this was brought on by the guilt she felt about murdering so many innocent people.

On 7 October 1968, construction workers repairing the floor above Delfina's cell accidentally dropped a bucket of cement on her head through a hole in the ceiling while she was in the middle of flirting with a woman prisoner who'd entered her cell.

Many believe Delfina was actually murdered on the orders of a co-operative of relatives of her victims, who'd sworn to get revenge on her for what she had done. Others believe that a number of the VIPs who used the sisters' brothels had decided their activities would be exposed unless she died.

Delfina's sister María Luisa González Valenzuela ('Eva the Leggy One') died alone in her cell at Irapuato jail on 19 November 1984. By the time prison staff discovered her body it had been virtually shredded by hungry rats.

The other sister María was sentenced to 25 years in prison and treated her enforced jail time with apparent disdain. She refused to talk to anyone about what she'd been found guilty of doing. She told one inmate she had no idea what her other sisters had been doing and didn't realise women had been murdered. A psychiatrist who examined María after she went to prison diagnosed her as suffering from classic self-denial.

María eventually met and fell in love with a 64-year-old male inmate in the same Irapuato prison and once both were released, they married and lived together in a life of complete obscurity, finally dying of old age in the mid 1990s. She was the only sister to survive her entire jail sentence and then be freed.

In 2002, workers clearing land for a new housing development in Purísima del Rincón, Guanajuato, down the road from the notorious Loma del Angel ranch, found the remains of 20 skeletons in a pit. Authorities said the victims were probably buried there on the orders of Delfina and María Torres.

If this is true, it raises the number of murders committed by the sisters to more than 110 people. This makes the sisters among the most prolific serial killers in history.

Despite the suffering they went through at the hands of their own father, they'd managed to overshadow his appalling catalogue of abuse by murdering dozens of innocent people. If only they'd come to terms with their childhoods then perhaps all this death and destruction could have been avoided.

CHAPTER FOUR

THE JUÁREZ SERIAL KILLER
ABDUL LATIF SHARIF

Abdul Latif Sharif's childhood played a pivotal role in shaping his entire life. He was the only child born into a Muslim family in Egypt on 19 September 1947 and his father was so controlling he even stopped his son from attending school. Family members later alleged that Abdul's father had recognised how intelligent his son was from an early age and wanted to stunt his development so he would never escape his twisted influence.

From the age of five, Abdul was sexually and physically abused by his father on virtually a daily basis. Abdul's only respite from these attacks was to train carrier pigeons in a small shed at the bottom of the garden of his home and occasionally fish on the bank of a nearby river. He later recalled there were many moments when he thought about jumping into the water, knowing he'd drown because he couldn't swim.

Back home he faced a never-ending catalogue of abuse at the hands of his father, while his timid, terrified mother hid in her bedroom to avoid the consequences of her husband's depraved actions. Abdul later said that he got so used to the abuse that he presumed all the other children in the world were treated just as badly. He saw it as some kind of sick initiation ceremony for the rest of his life.

Abdul found some measure of escape through reading books, most of which he hid from his father. He'd taught himself to read at the age of five and could devour an entire textbook in one sitting, even though he usually read in candlelight after his parents had gone to bed.

Abdul became fascinated by scientific books because they encouraged him to think more for himself. Eventually, he found himself able to calculate the scientific solutions to experiments before they'd been disclosed in many books.

In 1960 – at the age of just 12 – Abdul's father ordered him to marry his 10-year-old cousin. Both children were completely bemused by their hastily arranged wedding. Neither was mature enough to even know what sex meant, let alone that it could result in pregnancy.

Abdul's father insisted the pair lived at the family house and Abdul later told friends it was the most bewildering period of his already deeply disturbed life. His father would sit him and his child bride down, run through sex lessons and then insist on enacting everything out on the young couple. Neither dared to stand up to him for fear of being beaten and then banished from the house.

Abdul and his child bride were only ever allowed out to visit his wife's family home where they were permitted to watch television. He later recalled that America dominated most programmes and it seemed to him to be such a wonderful, liberating place compared to Egypt.

On one occasion, he naively risked the wrath of his controlling father by announcing that he'd like to travel to America one day. Abdul's father was so appalled that he urged his humourless sister – the mother of his young bride – to tell Abdul that he'd be cursed for ever if he and his young wife ever dared to leave Egypt.

Abdul's aunt (and mother-in-law) did, however, point out to her brother that his son needed to provide for her daughter, so he should allow him to attend school after all. Abdul was delighted and quickly caught up with the children of his own age at the school he attended. Teachers were particularly impressed by how good he was at science.

He poured himself into his school work as if his life depended on it. He saw it as an escape from being trapped at home. He even managed to avoid some of his father's never-ending assaults on him and his child bride by insisting he had to do his homework, otherwise he'd never be able to support them both when they had a family.

Abdul was so good at science that before he'd completed his final college entry exams, he was offered a place at Cairo University to study chemical engineering. But no one outside his family was aware of the horrors Abdul and his young wife were enduring back at home.

At university, Abdul – who was obliged to be a day student so he did not live away from home – earned an honours degree in chemical engineering after getting an average of 99 per cent on all the exams he took. It was an astonishing achievement for someone who hadn't been allowed to even go to school until the age of 12.

Abdul's family warned him, though, that he would have to continue living at their home with his wife, so he took a job as a science teacher at a local high school. He enjoyed his job but got bored quickly, and so some afternoons he'd slip into his old university laboratories to help academics from the science department to develop new drugs.

In 1970, Abdul's father was persuaded by one of his senior lecturers at the university to allow Abdul to travel to the Soviet Union on a scientific research trip. Abdul had been dreaming about such a journey ever since he was a child enduring his father's abuse on a daily basis. The urge to escape was powerful.

While in the Soviet Union, Abdul applied for a visa to travel to the US and headed straight to New York, where he immediately sought political asylum. Abdul was quickly granted legal status after revealing his academic qualifications and explaining his circumstances to US immigration officials. He found a job in the cosmetics and skin care industry thanks to his scientific background and settled in New York. Abdul seemed on the surface to be a professional, attractive and highly successful commercial scientist.

Abdul later recalled that, at first, New York women seemed to flock to him and he discovered many of them were very sexually liberated. It was a revelation to a small-town Egyptian, who'd been callously married off to his cousin at the age of 12.

With his thick dark hair and moustache, lean Abdul was considered quite a catch during his early days in America. He ended up marrying twice in a short period of time in New York but never admitted why the relationships broke down. He also went on to have at least five live-in relationships with other women. But his biggest love affair of all was with alcohol.

In 1978 – after eight years working in that job in New York – Abdul was fired for continually turning up at work drunk. He was also accused of stealing money from the company by falsifying his work expenses.

After being fired, Abdul moved to the rural community of New Hope, Pennsylvania, after getting a new job in a local cosmetics company. One of his friends at that time later recalled going on a deer-hunting trip with Abdul during which the Egyptian scientist shot and wounded a buck. He refused to finish off the dying animal with a bullet and instead crouched down next to it and pulled out a hunting knife. He then punctured its vital organs and watched the creature die a slow and agonising death.

Other friends and colleagues in Pennsylvania noticed that Abdul's girlfriends didn't last long and a few of them seemed to disappear at the end of each relationship. One of Abdul's friends even noticed a woman's possessions in a drawer at Abdul's home shortly after he'd split from yet another girlfriend. The friend claimed to have spotted a mud-caked shovel on the porch.

Whatever the truth about those missing girlfriends, Abdul recognised that it was time to move on before people started asking any awkward questions. So in 1981, he suddenly quit his job in Pennsylvania and moved to the warmer climes of Palm Beach, Florida, becoming employed as a scientific researcher at a well-known cosmetics company.

In Florida, Abdul married yet again. But the relationship quickly collapsed when his new wife walked out on him after he hit her. If his latest wife had filed a complaint at the time, then it's possible Abdul would have been stopped in his tracks. Instead, he started prowling singles bars in Miami looking for women to pick up.

Abdul's treatment of most women was by this time so inappropriate that they usually rejected his advances within moments of first meeting. One woman he tried to pick up in a bar later told how Abdul had tried to touch her breast after buying her a drink. Another one said that he asked her how often she liked sex after trying to ask her out on a date.

But while his personal relationships with women had become extremely disturbing, at work, Abdul gave off a completely different impression. His skills as a chemist and engineer were so highly valued that his new employer set up a department specifically for him and his own hand-picked team of researchers.

Despite all his success at work, the 'other side' of Abdul had evolved into being a promiscuous, secret alcoholic. And if he couldn't find a woman to have sex with, he'd turn to other ways to satisfy his urges. This included driving around the streets near his apartment picking up stray dogs and cats, which he took home and tortured, later saying that he found doing this sexually exciting. In the absence of real women, he also began collecting female clothes from laundries and stealing garments off clothes lines, which he took home to masturbate over.

Abdul later admitted that by this time he hated most women for rejecting him. Meanwhile his sexual urges became so uncontrollable that he began kerb-crawling around the seaside communities near his Florida home for prostitutes, whom he wanted to punish because of his resentment towards women.

Over the course of a few months, three sex workers complained to police about Abdul attacking them. He was arrested but avoided a jail sentence after his employers hired expensive lawyers to defend him because he was such a highly valued member of their scientific staff. While they did stand by him for a while, Abdul's bosses fired him in January 1982 after he was arrested by police for raping a woman who'd answered his advertisement for a housekeeper.

Abdul was held in Florida's Alachua County jail without bond pending a trial. He waited there until his court appearance a few days later. While being transferred by van to the court, he escaped from the vehicle when it stopped at traffic lights, but was on the run for just a few hours. He was cornered by police after being spotted in the backyard of a house trying to steal women's underwear from a washing line.

Back in prison on remand, Abdul insisted he was innocent and would be pleading not guilty. This held up the judicial process while prosecutors gathered evidence to back up the allegations which meant Abdul's trial wasn't held for another two years.

He was eventually found guilty and given a 12-year sentence for the rape. Prosecutors assured the judge that if and when Abdul was eventually released from prison he'd be 'met at the gates by US immigration officials and escorted to a plane' to be deported back to Egypt.

However, Abdul was freed in 1990 after less than five years for good behaviour and slipped out of the prison, completely ignoring the deportation order. He headed to Midland, Texas, where he was soon employed as a resident scientist by a research company. Even when Abdul was arrested for drunk driving, his deportation order still wasn't activated because of a breakdown in communications between the states of Florida and Texas.

Shortly after this, Abdul was accused of raping a woman he met in a bar. Once again, his defence costs were covered by his employers. But this time not even a skilful lawyer could help Abdul avoid being found guilty, although the judge inexplicably sentenced him to just two years in prison and he was eventually released on parole after serving just 12 months. But this time, the deportation order was finally activated and Abdul agreed to never set foot on American soil again.

But instead of Egypt, Abdul headed to the Mexican border city of Juárez where – in May 1994 – he was hired by one of his previous employer's associated corporations. The firm even rented Abdul a luxurious apartment in the exclusive Rincones de San Marcos district of Juárez.

This often chaotic Mexican city turned out to be an ideal hunting ground for the predatory Abdul thanks to its large population of young women who'd come from all over Mexico to work in the city's many shops and factories that had been set up specifically because of Juárez's close proximity to the US. Many of these factory workers – the factories known in Spanish as *maquiladoras* – were paid between $4 and $7 a day to assemble automotive parts and electronic components, and to manufacture cheap clothing.

This influx of mainly young women led to run-down shanty towns of small impromptu homes held together by flimsy wooden pallets, mattresses, cardboard boxes and baling wire springing up in Juárez. They usually contained no more than a bed and a tin washtub for bathing.

Just a few weeks after Abdul had arrived in Juárez, several young women were picked up on the city streets and murdered. Their bodies turned up in Lote Bravo, a sparsely populated desert region south of the city. A dozen more women disappeared under similar circumstances over the following 12 months.

In the middle of this crime spree, the 'other side' of Abdul continued to be a highly valued member of staff at the company where he worked as a residential scientist. He went on to patent a total of 25 new chemical formulas while working in Juárez, for which his employer was incredibly grateful.

In October 1995, a teenage *maquiladora* worker reported Abdul to the police for raping her at his home after she met him in a bar. The woman told police that Abdul had threatened to kill her and dump her body in Lote Bravo, where many of the other missing women's bodies had been discovered. But the charges against Abdul were eventually withdrawn following a secret 'compensation deal' between Abdul's employer and his accuser.

Days after the case was dropped, Juárez police uncovered evidence that Abdul had dated another teenage girl who'd been found raped and murdered in Lote Bravo, two months earlier in August 1995. Abdul was immediately arrested again and shortly after, Mexican prosecutors announced that they suspected Abdul had murdered at least 17 other young *maquiladora* workers who had disappeared over the previous 18 months since his arrival in Juárez.

Local newspapers and TV labelled Abdul as 'The Juárez Serial Killer' and law enforcement investigators assumed that, now he was behind bars, the murders would stop. But the corpses of more raped and strangled young women continued to be dumped in and around Juárez while Abdul remained locked up in prison awaiting trial. The police were stumped.

Under severe pressure from politicians, public officials and the media, Juárez police publicly alleged that Abdul had incited these new murders from inside prison by ordering and even paying other men in Juárez to continue the killing spree he began to ensure he was found innocent of the original murder charges.

There was no doubt Abdul was a sexual predator with a long history of assaulting women, but people questioned if he was really capable of ordering other people to kill innocent young females from inside his prison cell. Abdul reacted to the police allegations by inviting journalists to visit him in jail so he could inform them he had no connection to the men responsible for the numerous women found dead in Juárez. Abdul even claimed that before his arrest, he'd met one of the male suspects in a Juárez bar where he'd boasted about raping and murdering girls with the help of his cousin.

Abdul insisted to reporters that he was being deliberately blamed for the murders of the young women to cover up the identity of the real killers, who were politicians and local public dignitaries. Embarrassed by his public accusations, Mexican authorities immediately transferred Abdul to a more secure prison in Chihuahua and banned him from having any more media visits in jail. They refused to comment on his specific allegations.

Justice officials wouldn't allow Abdul to meet with his own lawyers to discuss his fast-approaching trial in case it affected the killings going on out in public. But when yet more women were murdered and raped in Juárez while Abdul was held in solitary confinement, it became clear Abdul wasn't the only serial killer in Juárez.

This was when the case against Abdul began to unravel. Abdul's lawyers received anonymous threats not to represent him and then the judge due to officiate at Abdul's trial on 18 murder charges admitted publicly that he didn't think there was enough evidence to actually find Abdul guilty.

Seventeen of the eighteen murder charges were suddenly dropped and Abdul was prosecuted for just one of the unsolved murders. He was convicted at his trial in March 1999 and received a 30-year sentence.

Despite only explicitly linking Abdul to one case, Juárez police continued to insist Abdul was a serial killer and this sole conviction did nothing to help solve the mystery of who had committed multiple serial killings in Juárez.

Weeks after Abdul's trial, city police reluctantly acknowledged that a total of 520 people had vanished over the previous three years and that 'an important percentage of them were female adolescents'.

* * *

Two months later – on 13 May 1999 – the son of Abdul's lawyer, Irene Blanco, was caught in the crossfire of a shoot-out between narco gangs. He'd been hit when rival gang members opened fire next to his car. Seriously injured, Eduardo had only just managed to drive himself to the nearest hospital.

Irene Blanco arrived there as her severely wounded son was being taken into an operating theatre. She heard agents from the state police ask the doctors whether her son would survive. Irene was left in no doubt that he had been shot because she represented alleged serial killer Abdul.

It was shortly after this that Juárez police arrested nine men for allegedly plotting with Abdul. Police alleged that the men were asked to murder numerous local women to make it look as if he was not the serial killer they'd insisted he was. Apparently several of the supposed killers visited Abdul in jail and had been paid by him to carry out the 'copycat' crimes.

One told police he'd collected 'a packet' from Abdul in prison that contained $4,000 in cash. But the same man later recanted his statement, scuppering the case, and eventually all the charges against Abdul and the other suspects were dropped. Despite this failure, Juárez police continued to publicly allege that Abdul and other men had conspired together to commit at least 17 of the murders that prosecutors had always blamed on Abdul.

While the case seemed to have disappeared, in late 1999 Abdul was charged with 24 counts of homicide plus dozens of kidnapping and rape charges, as well as being accused of organised crime and illegal human trafficking offences. But once again all charges against Abdul were dropped after a Juárez court ruled that there was insufficient evidence to uphold any of the accusations.

In February 2003, Abdul was awarded a judicial review of the single murder he'd earlier been found guilty of committing. The conviction was eventually upheld, although Abdul's 30-year sentence was cut to 20 and prosecutors once again publicly insisted Abdul was on the verge of being charged with additional murders.

Authorities in Juárez insisted they were determined Abdul should never be released from prison because they remained convinced he was a serial killer. However some victims' families suspected that he'd been conveniently linked to a number of other previously unsolved murders, which had no connection to him, to help the police clear up a host of unsolved murder cases. Then one prominent law and order official conceded that while Abdul was a serial killer, other individuals who'd murdered in a similar fashion remained on the loose in the city and may well have been responsible for some of the victims he had been accused of killing.

Abdul's alleged serial killings were never ultimately re-investigated because – having earlier been awarded the reduced sentence – he was diagnosed with cirrhosis of the liver which led to him getting hepatitis C. This worsened his ongoing condition of alcoholic hepatitis, and was all compounded by the major depressive disorder that doctors diagnosed at the time.

Abdul died on 2 June 2006, at the age of 59, in the Social Rehabilitation Center of Chihuahua prison, from a cardiac arrest generated by a chronic haemorrhage caused by peptic ulcer disease. He had not been prosecuted for any further murders following that original conviction but Juárez police insisted he had murdered dozens of women.

Abdul was buried in Mexico because no relatives could be found to repatriate his remains to Egypt. His funeral was attended by the Egyptian consul in Mexico, Karim El Sadat, who insisted Abdul was innocent of all the allegations against him.

Back in Juárez, more murders of young women were still being committed. Nearly all of them had a similar modus operandi to the early cases that were blamed on Abdul, with victims being snatched off the streets and their bodies then dumped on the outskirts of the city.

And the mystery deepened further when homicide detectives in Juárez revealed that their underworld sources had told them that Abdul was paid by the powerful Juárez drug cartel to deliberately organise the killings of many of the women from his prison cell in order to divert the police from cracking down on the drug trade. In a city like Juárez, drug cartels were certainly capable of such murderous manipulation but his death meant that there was no point in trying to prove these allegations.

Whatever the truth of the matter, Abdul's name will for ever be linked to the senseless murders of dozens of innocent young women. In all likelihood, he did indeed murder dozens of people but we will never know how many really died at his hands.

CHAPTER FIVE

THE GODFATHER OF MATAMOROS

ADOLFO DE JESÚS CONSTANZO

The Cuban quarter of Miami was a bustling place in the 1960s, as tens of thousands of refugees from the battle-ravaged Caribbean island arrived on flimsy boats trying to escape the rigid communist regime of Fidel Castro. Among them was recently widowed teenage mother Delia Aurora González del Valle and her baby son Adolfo de Jesús Constanzo. She'd been just 15 years old when he was born 18 months earlier.

They were desperately poor and ended up sleeping on the floor of a small one-storey house belonging to a cousin, who'd been living in Florida since the late 1950s. The American Dream must have seemed a million miles away for teenage mother Aurora and her infant son as they struggled to survive during those early months following their arrival in Miami in January 1964.

However, all this changed when pretty Aurora met a Puerto Rican immigrant who worked as a gardener in the affluent South Beach area of the city. She married him within months and happily agreed to move with him back to his home city of San Juan, Puerto Rico, a relief after her difficult experiences in the US.

In San Juan, the family had a modest but comfortable one-storey house on the edge of the city. Living costs were much lower than in the US, so Aurora found life much easier and, in many ways, it felt like Cuba to her.

Little Adolfo, now four years old, was baptised as a Catholic and attended a church school in San Juan. His mother was mightily proud when her young son was chosen by priests to serve the church as an altar boy.

Those who knew the family in San Juan later recalled that Adolfo almost always had a smile on his face whenever he was with his mother because he loved her so much. Aurora later explained that this was because of what they'd been through together.

But Aurora's new husband had to work long hours to ensure his wife and her child had a decent lifestyle, and his absences from the family home soon began to irritate domineering Aurora. She told one neighbour she missed Miami, despite all the difficulties she and Adolfo had experienced when they lived there. And when she heard that one of her cousins back in Florida was earning a huge salary compared to what her husband got in San Juan, she started to wonder if she'd made a big mistake moving to Puerto Rico.

The more her husband was away working, the more she wanted to be able to afford nice clothes and a bigger home.

The lure of Miami grew and grew and in the end she issued her husband with an ultimatum: either they all moved back to the US or she and Adolfo would go there on their own.

Desperate not to lose his wife, her husband reluctantly agreed to return to Miami. Adolfo was 10 years old when the family arrived back in the city, but the US economy in the early seventies was in trouble and Aurora's Puerto Rican husband struggled to find any work.

In the end, he had no choice but to start working for a gang of Cuban criminals. It was either that or his young family would starve or, at the very least, that Aurora would break up with him. Aurora had no idea at first that her husband had become a criminal. She was just happy to find them able to afford to live a much better lifestyle than they'd had in Puerto Rico.

Friends and neighbours of the family later recalled how Aurora seemed conveniently oblivious to her husband's nefarious activities. 'She shopped every single day and even went out dancing in the evenings with and without her husband,' one neighbour later recalled.

It was clear to many in the neighbourhood that Aurora was spending the money without a care for how much and how quickly he could make it. And in order to keep Aurora happy, her husband began to take some big risks inside the Miami underworld. So few were surprised when, just a year after the family had arrived back in Miami, Adolfo's stepfather died in a bloody shoot-out between rival gangs of drug dealers in the heart of the city's Little Cuba district.

Adolfo later recalled that his beloved mother didn't even seem particularly heartbroken when she heard he'd been killed. And at the funeral, Adolfo overheard relatives talking about how lucky Aurora was that he'd left her so much money.

She splashed out some of his illicit cash on purchasing a three-bedroomed detached house in one of Miami's best Cuban neighbourhoods. Aurora hadn't yet reached her thirties and she'd already been widowed twice. No wonder some of her friends and neighbours began referring to her as 'the merry widow'.

What her friends and relatives didn't know, though, was that Aurora had been hiding a secret vice for years. She'd been entrenched in the dark religious occult of Santería – the god of death – since long before the family fled Cuba more than 10 years earlier. And once Aurora and her mother had settled in their expensive new home, they set themselves up as *santeras*, or priestesses, of the cult. They had an altar specially built and openly worshipped at it most days.

After scouting around, Aurora soon discovered there were many potential disciples in the neighbourhood where she now lived. She began holding séances at the property, during which she claimed to be contacting the dead. Neighbours heard chanting and wailing coming from the house at all times of the day and night.

A lot of local residents began calling Aurora 'the witch' behind her back and many considered Santería to be nothing more than an evil, manipulative cult specifically aimed at taking advantage of vulnerable poor folk. When several neighbours complained to the police about the noisy activities, Aurora convinced cops who called at the house that others were simply jealous of her wealth following the death of her husband.

After the police left the house one evening, having agreed to take no further action against Aurora or her mother, she announced to her son Adolfo that she'd put a hex (a curse) on the neighbours who'd complained about her. When the same neighbours returned to the police to complain about Aurora's activities again a few nights later, she ordered the 12-year-old Adolfo to chop the heads off a couple of chickens and goats she'd just bought in the local butcher's and sling them on the neighbours' doorsteps in the middle of the night.

Adolfo later admitted he never questioned anything his mother ordered him to do. He even volunteered to buy live animals in the future and then kill them himself on the front porch to ensure that their neighbours thought Aurora and her son were 'truly evil'. Aurora was so impressed by Adolfo's enthusiasm that, despite his young age at the time, she anointed him as a Santería priest.

Adolfo embraced the movement and soon mother and son were travelling back and forth between Miami, Puerto Rico and Haiti, attending séances and other Santería events. These voodoo ceremonies often involved the sacrifice of live animals, although it all seemed perfectly normal to 13-year-old Adolfo.

* * *

As the 1970s continued in bustling Little Havana, Miami, Adolfo began to earn the status of high priest among his mother's many Santería disciples, who'd become regular visitors to their home. At the same time, Aurora used her supposed psychic powers and influence as a so-called Santería priestess to sleep with as many lovers as she wanted.

Adolfo later explained how he learned from an early age to divide the different 'compartments' of his life. He could switch from being a black magic priest into a studious, shy student at his local high school with relative ease.

Back at home, Adolfo's beloved mother was piling on weight, as she enjoyed a lavish lifestyle financed by the numerous cash donations from her many disciples. But as Aurora's weight ballooned, she began rarely leaving her house. Adolfo would be dispatched to do the shopping and other errands, though he was always under strict orders from his mother to come straight home afterwards.

Then suddenly Aurora stopped Adolfo attending school after one of his teachers turned up at the house to discuss an incident during which Adolfo had threatened to kill a classmate. No longer at school, Adolfo devoted even more of his time to assisting his mother during her séance sessions with the numerous disciples who visited the house.

One disciple announced to Adolfo one day that he was the boy's 'occult godfather'. The same man was one of Aurora's lovers and the teenager soon discovered that this Cuban-born man happened to be a trigger-happy gangster in the local drug trade.

Adolfo also heard rumours that this man had played a role in the murder of his stepfather, though he couldn't be entirely sure how true this was. The man regularly visited the house along with at least three of Aurora's other male lovers, all of whom were from the Cuban criminal community in Miami.

Adolfo's so-called occult godfather began pouring money into improvements inside the house, including converting the entire ground floor into a Santería church, complete with a new altar and even bench seats for disciples to sit on during services.

Aurora's generous lover was eventually anointed an occult priest with her full approval. However, he shamelessly used this new status to go to bed with many of the women disciples who visited the church. Sometimes he even shared them with Aurora. If any of the couple's lovers dared to question their sexual demands, then they'd be encouraged to consume huge amounts of narcotics that the new priest supplied to make them more compliant.

A couple of these female disciples later claimed they were threatened by Aurora and her lover that if they didn't sleep with them then they'd be cursed. Despite all this, there was no shortage of Santería followers among the poorer residents of Miami's Little Havana who would follow the church's orders.

Witnessing all this was teenage Adolfo. He later recalled that the behaviour of his mother and her occult priest lover seemed 'fine' to him at the time. Following in their footsteps, and becoming more immersed in the ideals of Santería, he started using his supposedly special 'powers' to persuade younger women disciples to sleep with him as well.

Aurora further enhanced her teenage son's reputation as a priest with psychic powers by proudly announcing to her disciples that Adolfo had predicted many world events, including the 1981 shooting of then president Ronald Reagan.

If Adolfo and his free-spending mother ever got low on cash, they'd go out shoplifting for food and clothes in the centre of Miami. The pair ended up being arrested several times for petty crimes, such as theft, vandalism and shoplifting. One of the items Adolfo was accused of stealing was a chainsaw. Both mother and son pleaded poverty to prosecutors and managed to avoid custodial jail sentences.

It was around this time that Aurora's lover started teaching Adolfo the skills required to be a drug dealer and con artist. He called it a career in 'profiting from evil', and it certainly seemed a lot less risky than shoplifting.

When Adolfo Constanzo reached 18 years of age, his now medically obese mother ordered him to begin studying the Afro-Caribbean religion of Palo Mayombe with a local high priest recently arrived from Cuba. Whereas practitioners of Santería sacrificed animals for their rituals, Palo Mayombe encouraged the use of actual human parts, often stolen from graves.

There were rumours in Little Havana that the Palo Mayombe priest training Adolfo would sacrifice living people on altars, if they were perceived to be possessed by the Devil. But before the now tall and handsome Adolfo had an opportunity to put his new Palo Mayombe 'skills' to the test, he was approached by a modelling agent on the streets of Miami Beach. Adolfo was outside a department store about to go in and shoplift some clothes at the time.

The talent spotter persuaded Adolfo to go back with her to a nearby photographic studio to pose for photos. Within weeks, Adolfo was getting regular work as a male model on professional photo shoots. Back home, his mother was delighted by the extra money her son was earning. And for the first time in his entire life, Adolfo was not being controlled by Aurora, so he felt a certain freedom too. While working as a male model, Adolfo began sleeping with lovers of both sexes. He particularly liked the way that his new career enabled him to more openly flaunt his preference for men, without being treated as some kind of sexual weirdo.

Back home, Adolfo's controlling mother Aurora was so overweight she was now forced to attend her black magic services in a wheelchair steered by her son or one of her lovers. As a result of his mother's disability, Adolfo was obliged to continue practising as a high priest whether he liked it or not. However, he was very careful to keep his occult activities secret from his colleagues in the glamorous world of modelling.

* * *

In 1983, a photographic assignment took Adolfo to Mexico City. He knew Mexicans were extremely receptive to practices such as Santería so he saw the visit as a perfect opportunity to spread the word about his occult beliefs. During his stay in the city, Adolfo spent much of his free time wandering around the gay district of Zona Rosa offering to read strangers' fortunes with tarot cards.

Adolfo later said he felt much more at home in Mexico City than anywhere else he'd ever been. People seemed prepared to take Santería and Palo Mayombe much more seriously than they did back in Miami.

During the same modelling assignment in Mexico City, Adolfo picked up his first two Mexican disciples; a gay psychic called Martín Quintana Rodríguez and a handsome youth called Omar Orea Ochoa. They both told Adolfo they'd been obsessed with the occult from an early age. Adolfo seduced both men and even insisted they role-play men and women in bed, depending on his sexual mood. Quintana and Orea didn't object in the slightest, so enamoured were they by handsome Adolfo.

On Adolfo's return to Miami, he found himself pining for his two lovers, as well as the life of relative freedom he'd enjoyed during that brief visit to Mexico City. However, Aurora and her drug-dealing lover had other things on their minds. They insisted that, with Adolfo now a fully-fledged Palo Mayombe priest, they needed to find some live humans to sacrifice. Adolfo pointed out that their ongoing disputes with neighbours might make that a very risky activity, so they agreed to stick to animal sacrifices for the moment. One night, the local police appeared at Aurora's Miami house and warned Adolfo to stop leaving the remains of dead animals on their neighbours' doorsteps, otherwise he'd be arrested.

Around this time, out in the centre of Miami, Adolfo suffered several vicious homophobic and racist attacks. He refused to hide his sexuality and some of Aurora's disciples began questioning Adolfo's suitability as a black magic priest because he was so openly gay.

Aurora had ignored her son's sexual preferences and told him she didn't care who he slept with as long as he stayed with her. He later said he felt stifled inside the house, unable to express his true feelings, which made him desperate to escape his mother's toxic influence. So, despite the pleas of his housebound, clinically obese mother, Adolfo moved to Mexico City full-time after telling her he was sick of living in 'straight' America. Following Adolfo's move to Mexico City in the middle of 1984, his mother told all her disciples that her son had gone to a special retreat in Mexico to 'cleanse his soul'.

In Mexico City, Adolfo immediately moved into an apartment with his two male lovers Quintana and Orea, whom he'd met during that earlier modelling shoot. They formed an open ménage à trois which usually meant sharing a bed together.

Adolfo had presumed he'd continue to get modelling assignments, but there wasn't as much work in Mexico City, so he decided to concentrate on his 'skills' as a black magic, tarot-reading priest instead. Wherever Adolfo went, he would see evidence of Mexico's fascination with dark religious beliefs, influenced by a crossover of Christianity and other ancient religions, and he found many specialised stores there that openly sold powerful toxic herbs, potions and amulets.

And these dark practices extended out far beyond Mexico City. Police officers and other law enforcement agents – especially in the *campo* (countryside) areas – hung strings of garlic and even peppers in their police stations, and white candles were lit in people's homes to ward off evil.

Brujos, or shamans (priests), worked in many *pueblos* (villages) across the nation, casting spells while relieving disciples of small fees. Even in vast metropolises like Mexico City, superstitions were a way of life for many; one *maquiladora* (factory) managed to avoid a government safety inspector's shutdown order when a *curandero* (cleaner) used herbs and spiritualism to dehex a piece of expensive machinery, which had seriously injured a worker in an industrial accident.

In 1980s Mexico even the plot of hugely popular TV soap opera, *El Maleficio* ('The Evil One') revolved around the premise that a wealthy businessman was able to sustain power by praying nightly to Satan. All this meant that, back on the streets of Mexico City's predominantly gay Zona Rosa, Adolfo quickly picked up more new disciples through his tarot card readings. In addition, he offered *limpias* – ritual cleansings – for those convinced they'd been cursed by their enemies.

Adolfo utilised the drug-dealing training he'd received from his mother's underworld lover back in Miami to nurture narcos as customers because they had plenty of cash and a lot of evil spirits to 'cleanse'. These gangsters soon began asking Adolfo's advice on drug shipments and transactions, believing his special predictive powers could protect their criminal activities.

Adolfo launched an additional 'service' which involved casting magic spells to make his drug-dealer disciples and their *sicarios* (hit men) invisible to police. He assured his disciples they would be literally bulletproof whenever they came up against their enemies.

Many of these criminals came from dirt-poor Mexican peasant stock and had been raised to believe in the power of the Santería and Palo Mayombe occult movements, which had evolved via the slave trade in Cuba. Because of this, most of these disciples never questioned anything that Adolfo told them. After all, he was a *brujeria* – high priest. He had the power they required to rule the underworld.

Within a couple of months of arriving in Mexico City, Adolfo had at least 30 drug-dealer disciples paying him as much as $4,500 each to hold occult ceremonies on their behalf. Most were armed with Uzi sub-machine guns and drove armour-plated limousines and pickup trucks.

In order to warrant charging such high fees, Adolfo developed a new 'show' for his underworld disciples, during which he sacrificed live animals in order to further convince the narcos of his black magic powers. Adolfo's events included a special 'menu' entitled 'sacrificial beasts'. Killing live roosters cost $6 a head, goats were $30, boa constrictors $450, adult zebras $1,100, and African lion cubs listed at $3,100 each.

It's never been disclosed how he got his hands on some of the rarer breeds, but disciples present at these ceremonies later alleged that every type of animal was sacrificed. After these impressive displays, Adolfo's narco disciples began demanding that he stepped up to another level.

Seeing the potential to earn even more cash, Adolfo and two of his most loyal disciples raided a Mexico City graveyard and stole some human remains, which enabled him to qualify as an *nganga* (spiritual priest). The ceremonies using human remains were very impressive to his rich criminal disciples and even more drug dealers began joining Adolfo's religious clan. He astutely encouraged an air of mystery and danger around himself and this ensured that few of them dared question his qualifications as a high priest.

Meanwhile, word was spreading across a wide cross section of Mexico City society that Adolfo's occult practices were powerful and effective for people from all walks of life. Adolfo's handsome features certainly helped further convince people he was not a charlatan. As he later explained: 'If I'd been ugly and seedy-looking, they might have questioned my practices, but instead they seemed to accept every word I said.'

New disciples included physicians, real estate tycoons, fashion models and even several transvestite nightclub performers. Adolfo supplied many of his more artistic disciples with drugs, which he claimed would help enhance their 'connection' to his voodoo practices.

Eventually, several top-ranking police and government officials began consulting Adolfo about his 'services' to benefit their own personal lives. Allegedly, this included at least four members of Mexico's Federal Judicial Police – known as the 'Federales'. They were said to have paid as much as $8,000 each to attend Adolfo's ritual 'cleansings', which they believed would ensure them a happy and prosperous life.

One of the senior police officers involved was a commander in charge of Mexico City's narcotics squad. To this day, no one knows if he took any drugs supplied by Adolfo but there are multiple allegations that he regularly attended his ceremonies. Another alleged disciple was a renowned police investigator who'd just retired from the *Federales* to lead the Mexican branch of Interpol – the European-wide police agency – to assist in the global fight against narcotics.

Mexico is a country where bribery – known as *mordida* – has existed across all levels of law enforcement for generations. Several federal officers even worked as trigger men (*sicarios*) for drug cartels but, despite this, the involvement of senior police officers with Adolfo was still very disturbing. Adolfo believed that these powerful law enforcement disciples would probably do anything he and his drug gangster clients asked of them once they'd joined his occult clan.

In the summer of 1986, one of Adolfo's male lovers, Florentino Ventura, introduced Adolfo to the notorious Calzada crime family, who at that time ran one of Mexico's most powerful drug cartels. Adolfo quickly impressed the hard-nosed Calzada clan with his unique combination of charm and black magic rituals. Members of the cartel soon began paying huge fees to be empowered by Adolfo in carefully orchestrated ceremonies. The primary preoccupation of the Calzada family members was to avoid being killed or arrested.

By early 1987, Adolfo was earning enough money from his richest followers to buy hundreds of thousands of dollars' worth of luxury cars, as well as a condominium in Mexico City. The cars included a Mercedes-Benz limousine that cost more than $250,000. Adolfo was also spending tens of thousands of dollars every month maintaining his luxurious lifestyle.

Throughout this period, he continued to devise increasingly outrageous 'black magic ceremonies' to earn more money and attract disciples. By this time, no one ever questioned his motives when it came to using animals and human corpses stolen from cemeteries during sacrificial ceremonies.

But keeping up the act was hard work, and a lot of Adolfo's seemingly natural confidence and hyperactivity at this time was being fuelled by his own addiction to cocaine. This encouraged him to completely ignore the consequences of his actions and believe he could get away with anything.

So he kept using the human remains he stole from local cemeteries during sacrifices and at one point, he was so confident of his own powers of persuasion that he posed as a DEA agent to rip off a cocaine baron in the city of Guadalajara. He then sold the stolen narcotics through his black magic police contacts for $100,000. Adolfo went out of his way to convince the notorious Calzada drug cartel that his magical powers were responsible for much of their own runaway success and survival.

In April 1987, Adolfo visited the two brothers who headed up the crime family and demanded an equal partnership in the syndicate. The family were stunned by Adolfo's suggestion and immediately turned him down. However, they tried to soften the blow of their rejection by explaining they had a policy of only allowing their own relatives to sit at the top table of the cartel.

Adolfo gritted his teeth, furious they'd rejected his approach. He decided for the moment to appear to take their decision in his stride, although beneath the surface, Adolfo wanted to show the Calzadas he was someone not to cross.

Two weeks later – on 30 April 1987 – overall cartel chief Guillermo Calzada and six members of his gang vanished minutes after they'd left their Mexico City headquarters. The gangsters had been snatched off the street by Adolfo and his disciples. They were tied up and driven to an isolated warehouse where Adolfo and his clan shot them all dead. Afterwards, their bodies were cut into small pieces before being turned into a bloody cauldron of stew by Adolfo. He later claimed that he needed the blood to further build up his own strength to ensure he destroyed the entire cartel for daring to reject him. His plan was to shut the whole family down permanently.

Twenty-four hours after the kidnappings, other senior members of the Calzada family reported the disappearances to corrupt officers inside the city's police department. Detectives who searched the cartel headquarters noticed melted candles and other evidence of a religious ceremony in the main office. Cartel chiefs insisted the paraphernalia had no connection to the disappearances of the gangsters. Over the following few days, the family's corrupt police officers continued searching high and low for the missing gangsters completely unaware of their actual fate.

Six days after the original incident, police officers fished the mutilated remains of one of the missing cartel members out of the Zumpango River, located close to the gang's headquarters.

Within a week, police had recovered the mutilated corpses of the remaining five missing members of the cartel. They had all been sadistically tortured, with fingers, toes and ears removed. The bodies also had hearts and sex organs ripped out. Part of the spine had been removed from one corpse and two others were missing their brains.

But the grisly discovery of those body parts backfired on Adolfo. He'd presumed his plans for murderous intimidation of the rest of the cartel would force them into a humiliating surrender, but it had actually made him the most marked man in Mexico City. Other vengeful members of the Calzada family were out looking for him, so Adolfo abandoned the city and headed for the town of Matamoros, on the border with Texas. It was in a sparsely populated region where Adolfo believed he could launch his own cartel by joining forces with local drug gangsters. They'd form a protective ring of steel around him while he converted them into fully-fledged followers of Palo Mayombe.

Adolfo had learned from his childhood experiences back in Miami that drugs and black magic were a potent combination. He had grandiose plans to rule the underworld.

* * *

In July 1987, in Matamoros, one of Adolfo's male lovers, Salvador García, introduced him to a narco family led by brothers Elio and Ovidio Hernández. They wanted Adolfo to use his 'powers' to make them and their henchmen even more invincible and they happily agreed to welcome him into their cartel. It was exactly what Adolfo had wanted.

The Hernández brothers believed they needed spiritual protection for their cartel from law enforcement and their underworld enemies. Witches and *curanderos* were about to become as much a part of the Hernández's daily lives as lawyers and doctors were for other criminals. Adolfo anointed himself the Hernández gang's high priest after they agreed to pay him a cut of their drug trade because they were so impressed with his black magic credentials.

Adolfo quickly began using a wide range of Santería, Palo Mayombe and old fashioned voodoo rituals to keep his new gangster disciples happy. He encouraged the Hernández brothers and their gang to smoke ritual cigars, drink ritual rum and slaughter ritual chickens and goats. They even agreed to pray to various deities including Oshun, the god of money and sex.

Adolfo insisted that all the Hernández gang members called him 'El Padrino' – the Godfather – one part of his introduction of various forms of mind control in the guise of religious mumbo jumbo. Adolfo's new base in Matamoros was ideal because it meant he was on 'call' for the Hernández brothers and their gang of outlaws, whose ranch headquarters was located just 25 miles outside the city.

In Matamoros, Adolfo also expanded his own narcotics operation in the city, as well as getting a reputation as a much-feared *mayombero*, which ensured that rival drug dealers were terrified of him. All this further endeared him to the Hernández brothers.

* * *

On 30 July 1987, Adolfo Constanzo was driving his latest brand-new Mercedes through Matamoros when he narrowly avoided a collision with a motorist. Adolfo got out to apologise to the driver, an unusually tall, masculine-looking 22-year-old Mexican woman called Sara Aldrete. He later recalled there was an instant chemistry between them, especially when he discovered that Aldrete's birthday was the same as his mother's.

Aldrete was a Mexican national with resident alien status in the United States, where she attended college in Brownsville, Texas. In fact, the near miss involving Sara Aldrete had been no accident. She'd earlier been encouraged by one of Adolfo's disciples she met in a bar to join Adolfo's clan and had been following him when the accident occurred.

They went for a coffee together and Adolfo told his new friend that in his tarot cards he could see she was sad about the break-up of her most recent relationship. He also told her she'd been extremely lucky to walk away unscathed from such a toxic affair.

The pair slept together within hours of meeting, though it was only a brief affair as Adolfo made no secret of his preference for men. But while their sexual relationship ended, Adolfo and Aldrete's friendship endured.

Within months, Aldrete had become Adolfo's closest confidante. He even began calling her 'La Madrina', 'the Godmother'. Adolfo later admitted he adored Aldrete because she didn't seem to have a conscience and she never once tried to get him to change any of his increasingly bloody sacrificial practices.

Adolfo's rituals became even more sadistic after he and Aldrete and his other disciples moved to the Hernández gang's Rancho Santa Elena, in the desert 25 miles outside Matamoros. Now based on the isolated compound, it quickly became clear that the Hernández brothers expected Adolfo to increase the number of his occult rituals to ensure even stronger spiritual protection for their drug gang.

Adolfo recognised that he needed to devise even more graphic services to guarantee the Hernández brothers never turned their backs on him and his disciples. He told Sara Aldrete that they needed to find the perfect human specimens for sacrifices.

On 28 May 1988, Adolfo shot dead a drug dealer called Hector de la Fuente and a farmer named Moises Castillo on the outskirts of the ranch compound. Their bullet-riddled corpses were then used as human sacrifices to impress the Hernández brothers and their gang members.

Adolfo knew his obsession with torturing and killing people would ensure that the Hernández brothers and their gangsters would be even less likely to question his spiritual abilities. Adolfo assured them that extreme mutilation was an essential ingredient of Palo Mayombe. He also insisted that all the blood and viscera from those victims would help feed the *nganga*, which he manipulated with sticks in front of his disciples as he claimed to be tuning into the spirit world.

Adolfo – now the all-powerful presiding priest or *mayombero* at the ranch – further proved he was possessed by the spirits by blowing cigar smoke and spitting liquor at the corpse of his victims before assuring his flock of followers at the ranch that all human sacrifices 'must die screaming', even if they were already dead.

Adolfo then laid out his favourite sacrificial weapons including a horseshoe, a chain and lethal-looking railroad spikes before sodomising the corpses of the two men. He even announced to his disciples that having sex with the bodies was his right as a god. Afterwards, he slashed their remains into tiny pieces.

Alongside Adolfo throughout the rituals was his number one disciple Sara Aldrete, now fully anointed as the cult's *madrina*. He encouraged her to come up with new ways to torture sacrificial victims and both agreed that from now on many of them would still be alive when they were dragged up to the altar.

And in the middle of all this frenzied murder and mayhem, Sara Aldrete continued living a bizarre double life as an honours student at a college just across the border in the US. Each evening, Aldrete would drive back over the international bridge in her new Ford Taurus to join Adolfo praying before his blood-splattered altar as killings and other rituals were performed. Witnesses later alleged that Aldrete always had a look of hollow detachment on her face while atrocities were carried out in front of her.

She and Adolfo even began using the 1987 horror film *The Believers*, starring Martin Sheen and directed by John Schlesinger, to try and keep all their disciples onside. The film centred on a cult in New York City that conducted human sacrifices in order to make money.

Sara Aldrete also allegedly took part in capturing human sacrifices by luring them into one of the ranch's outbuildings, often with the promise of sex. Later, she'd supervise the slow and painful death of each victim. This often included cutting off nipples with scissors and then draining the blood from each wound into a cup. The victim would eventually be boiled alive in a cauldron of steaming hot blood and water in front of the altar.

A lot of the victims were actually rival drug dealers lured to the ranch. Others were dirty cops who'd either gone back on an agreement or demanded more money from the Hernández brothers.

Adolfo involved the two gangsters closely in his ceremonies by anointing them as executioner priests. This involved branding their arms, chests and backs with a red-hot knife to ensure they fully appreciated their full membership of his cult.

One rival gangster at this time was dragged up to the main altar by three disciples and had his heart cut out by Adolfo while he was still alive. Many working on the property later said they could hear the man's screams ringing through the darkness.

The Hernández brothers then urged Adolfo to agree that their next victim should be a specific Matamoros cop who'd upset the gang. He was lured to the ranch, but when the chosen officer arrived at the main farmhouse, he immediately realised what was happening and reached for his gun. He had to be shot dead on the spot before the sacrificial ceremony could begin, and the sudden and untimely death left Adolfo, Sara Aldrete and the two Hernández brothers without a live victim to sacrifice.

So the brothers sent three henchmen out to grab the first person they could find on the flatlands surrounding the property. This turned out to be a teenage boy looking for his lost goat on a nearby prairie. He was dragged screaming up to the altar and boiled alive in front of the disciple gangsters.

His remains and those of most victims of the cult were buried in and around a steep corral behind an outhouse on the perimeter of the ranch. The Hernández brothers believed that using live humans would help intimidate their own gang members into remaining entirely loyal to them.

After at least a dozen murders at the ranch, Adolfo announced that he and Sara Aldrete required a better cross section of victims, so he was going to Mexico City to find some more to bring to the ranch. At first, the brothers were not happy with this plan, but Adolfo persuaded them it was essential for their spiritual powers. They stepped aside and Adolfo and Aldrete set off back to Mexico City in mid July 1988.

Within hours of them arriving in Adolfo's favourite area of Zona Rosa, he and his disciples had dismembered a transvestite called Ramon Esquivel and dropped his body parts into a cauldron of boiling hot water. The remains of Esquivel's corpse were then dumped on a nearby street corner.

Adolfo felt so energised by this sacrifice in Mexico City that he decided to pull off a big drugs deal while he was there. He approached a local cartel with a proposition to purchase a large shipment of cocaine from them and ended up taking the drugs without paying for them. Then he headed to Houston, Texas, to sell the cocaine to a gang for hundreds of thousands of dollars.

Just as the handover was taking place, a Houston police SWAT team came crashing in through the front door. Adolfo only just managed to escape out of a back door as the cops surged through the house.

Investigators searching the property uncovered some of Adolfo's occult paraphernalia, which he'd used to convince the gang to do business with him. The cocaine sold to the gang by Adolfo turned out to be one of Houston's biggest-ever drug hauls, but detectives were never able to formally identify the man who'd fled as they raided the house.

Back at the apartment in Mexico City where he was staying with Sara Aldrete and his two male lovers, Adolfo maniacally announced he felt as invincible as ever. While he may have felt unstoppable, his around-the-clock consumption of cocaine was, by this time, starting to impact his activities. He was barely sleeping and becoming increasingly trigger-happy and very paranoid.

* * *

On 12 August 1988, Hernández's brother Ovidio and his two-year-old son were kidnapped as they drove across the rocky flatlands that surrounded the family ranch near Matamoros. A rival cartel informed his brother that they'd snatched the pair as revenge for an $800,000 drug rip-off organised by the Hernández clan. The family immediately appealed to Adolfo for help and he agreed to return from Mexico City.

Adolfo believed that if he safely rescued Ovidio and his son, the brothers would reward him with an even more powerful position inside the cartel. He quickly established the names of the specific criminals who'd carried out the original kidnap and the ringleader was snatched off the streets of a local town.

The man was immediately taken to the Hernández ranch and burned alive in front of Adolfo's disciples. News of the killing reached the rival cartel who'd ordered the kidnapping and within hours Ovidio and his son were released unharmed.

Adolfo understandably claimed full credit for their safe return and the Hernández gang rewarded him with a more hands-on day-to-day role inside the cartel's core drug business. Adolfo threw himself into the Hernández's narco trade with such intensity that little else seemed to matter to him by this time.

When he was told that one of his old male lovers had committed suicide in Mexico City after shooting his wife and a friend dead, he just shrugged his shoulders and blamed the tragedy on the man's excessive cocaine consumption. Sara Aldrete later claimed, though, that this was a wake-up call for Adolfo, who actually quit taking cocaine soon afterwards, and in October 1988 Adolfo announced to his disciples that he was instigating a ban on the use of all narcotics on the ranch and anyone who defied his orders would be shot.

A few weeks later, a 35-year-old ex-cop and cult member called Jorge Valente de Fierro Gomez was caught snorting a line of cocaine on the ranch. Gomez was dragged on to the altar in one of the outhouses and then forced to endure a long and painful death inside a cauldron of boiling water. As Adolfo encircled the cauldron, he chanted that Gomez was an offering to Kadiempembe, the ultimate mystical devil of the Palo Mayombe religion.

Around the same time, one of the Hernández gang's drug smugglers, Ezequiel Rodríguez Luna, was targeted by Adolfo, who suspected Luna of betraying the cartel. He was tortured in front of disciples on the ranch until he admitted to selling drugs to a rival cartel. He was then shot in the head by Adolfo and his body drained of blood. The corpse itself was cut into small pieces.

The following day, two rival cartel members – Ruben Vela Garza and Ernesto Rivas Diaz – were killed by half a dozen of the Hernández brothers' henchmen during a shoot-out on the outskirts of the ranch. The bodies of the two men were then drained of blood and the remains cut into small pieces by Adolfo and his disciples.

One disciple later recalled that such murders had become perfectly 'normal' by this time. 'We were all in a sense hypnotised by Adolfo, Sara and their closest disciples, who were running our entire lives.'

Nine days later, Adolfo and his disciples kidnapped a man found wandering near the ranch. He was never identified. They planned to sacrifice him alive but the man put up such a fight that Adolfo had to order a Hernández henchman to shoot him before the customary rituals and torture could begin.

On 25 February 1989, a couple of Adolfo's most loyal disciples kidnapped a 14-year-old boy they found wandering on the deserted prairie north of the ranch. They presumed he was a spy working for a rival cartel, even though he strongly protested his innocence.

After throwing a gunnysack over the boy's head, the henchmen dragged him to the ranch's main altar where Elio Hernández and Adolfo were waiting with Sara Aldrete.

Hernández immediately decapitated the boy with a machete, never even bothering to lift the sack covering his face.

As the headless body flopped down on the floor next to the altar, Hernández noticed the boy's grey-and-green football jersey. He hesitantly leaned down and emptied the sack containing the head. He'd just executed his own nephew, schoolboy José García.

The death of the teenager completely freaked out the Hernández brothers, who convinced themselves they would be destined for hell because of what had happened. Adolfo assured them this was not the case, as the target was nothing more than collateral damage to the larger cause. But both brothers warned Adolfo that from now on, he could only sacrifice strangers.

On 13 March 1989 – just two weeks after the murder of the Hernández nephew – Adolfo sacrificed another living person at the ranch's altar. This time, Adolfo made sure he was a complete stranger with no connection to the cartel.

This latest victim didn't scream and plead for mercy like most did, which irritated Adolfo, as he later admitted he always preferred it when they fought back. Adolfo had clearly grown a chilling thirst for blood and, to the other cartel members, the murders seemed to be increasingly being committed on the spur of the moment and often for no apparent reason.

Adolfo would order his disciples to go and find him what he referred to as 'fresh meat' on virtually a daily basis. One day he told them he wanted an 'Anglo' man for his next ritual. In other words, a white person.

So on a Saturday in the middle of March 1989, a gang of Adolfo's most loyal disciples headed to the nearby border community of Matamoros. The town's bars were crammed with American teenagers on drinking sprees enjoying their college spring break.

* * *

Just before midnight, American student Mark Kilroy and his friends left the Hard Rock bar on the town's Calle Alvaro Obregon. They were walking back towards their cars parked on the other side of a nearby bridge when they noticed a Latino man in his twenties watching them from the pavement.

As Kilroy stopped to urinate against a nearby tree, one of his friends saw the same man walking towards Kilroy as if he knew him. After looking ahead to see where they were going next, his friend looked back in Kilroy's direction. He'd vanished.

The three teenagers searched the surrounding scrubland but there wasn't a trace. One of them later said it was as though Mark Kilroy had evaporated in the darkness.

In fact, Adolfo's disciples had grabbed Kilroy in the shadows as his friends walked ahead of them. They'd immediately gagged him and dragged him to a Chevy Suburban SUV parked close by and thrown him in the back seat.

After the vehicle had travelled a few blocks through Matamoros's deserted streets, one of Adolfo's disciples pulled up to relieve himself in an alleyway. Kilroy kicked one of his captors in the groin and managed to scramble out of the SUV.

As he ran down the empty, badly lit street, Adolfo's gangster disciples fired up the Suburban and gave chase. They eventually cornered Kilroy down a nearby alleyway and dragged him back to the truck. But this time he was handcuffed and ordered to lie on the floor in the back of the vehicle. The disciples then drove south on the back streets of Matamoros before passing an abandoned industrial estate, which bordered acres of planted fields that stretched off into the distant *campo* beyond the town.

The hot, sticky country air that night smelt musty and overused. One of the disciples later recalled that Kilroy kept asking why they'd taken him. He could see and hear that his kidnappers were all about his own age.

Eventually, the SUV turned off the main highway on to a narrow dirt track that snaked between two vast cornfields. For at least five miles, the Suburban bounced and squeaked its way through the darkness before its headlights illuminated a barn and other outhouses in the distance. On one side of the track was an irrigation levee. Beyond it were the rusting, abandoned remains of farm equipment scattered along the other side of the same track.

The Suburban slid to a halt in the dust. Adolfo's disciples got out and locked the truck, leaving Mark Kilroy handcuffed in the back. He didn't see any of them again that night.

At dawn, an elderly farm caretaker appeared alongside the car with a plate of eggs, bread and a bottle of water. He opened the back door, sat him up on the rear floor of the truck and awkwardly spoon-fed the American student. Afterwards, the caretaker locked the car door and disappeared in the direction of an outhouse.

Much later that same morning – at least 12 hours after Kilroy's original abduction – Adolfo and his disciples appeared by the car. They wrapped duct tape around Kilroy's head and over his eyes and mouth before pulling him roughly out of the car. With his hands still cuffed behind his back, they pushed him across a dusty courtyard.

When Kilroy tried to break free, three of the gang tackled him to the ground and then dragged him by the ankles across the dusty yard towards a large tin shed on the perimeter of the ranch.

Inside the crumbling old building were the remains of what looked like some kind of altar built on a chipped concrete floor. The air inside smelt like rotting meat. Surrounding the altar were black candles, cigar butts and half-empty bottles of a cheap cane liquor known as *aguardiente*.

Alongside this were also white candles, peppers and small pods of garlic that had been left earlier by a so-called white magician brought in by Adolfo to purify the site following a particularly bloody sacrifice. Next to the altar was a machete.

On a small, old-fashioned wood-burning cooker nearby were two cooking pots. They contained chicken and goat heads, plus thousands of penny coins, some crunched up bits of bones and strings of gold beads.

There was also a big iron kettle with a cluster of wooden stakes sticking out of it. The stakes were stained with the remnants of congealed blood, as well as fragments of human and animal body parts.

As the young American student was dragged up to the front of the altar, Adolfo stepped out from the shadows behind it. With three disciples struggling to keep Kilroy quiet, Adolfo looked straight at him and said a brief prayer.

When the prayer was finished, Adolfo slowly picked up the machete leaning against the side of the altar. He grasped it carefully with both hands for a few more moments. Then, without uttering a word, he swiped it through the air with such precision that Kilroy's entire head was chopped off in a nanosecond.

Adolfo and his disciples gathered hungrily around the decapitated corpse and began stabbing it maniacally with knives. Then they used their bare hands to gauge out the victim's brains, heart and lungs.

Mark Kilroy's bloody testicles were dropped in the iron kettle as part of a special brew, which was then passed around among the disciples to drink. Adolfo assured them they would 'be sanctified' by what they consumed.

* * *

Thirty miles away, police on both sides of the US/Mexico border, weren't particularly concerned when Kilroy's friends reported him missing. They pointed out to them that many young Americans had in the past disappeared for a few hours after drinking too much. They usually reappeared with ferocious hangovers and no memory of what had happened the night before.

But when there was no sign of Kilroy for the entire day after his disappearance, his friends returned to the Mexican police and pleaded with them to help. Officers conceded that perhaps there had been foul play but there were so no solid leads so they didn't know where or how to begin their investigation.

A few days after Kilroy's murder – in late March 1989 – Mexican authorities began carrying out one of their periodic anti-drug operations, erecting roadblocks and sweeping the border areas for unwary smugglers. On 9 April, a relative of the Hernández brothers drove through one of those police roadblocks without stopping.

The driver had believed Adolfo's pledge that he would be invisible to the police, thanks to all those live sacrifices at the altar on the ranch. So he was very surprised when officers in a squad car started chasing him towards Matamoros.

When the police finally forced the man's car to stop, he bizarrely invited officers to shoot him, convinced that Adolfo's powers would ensure the bullets would bounce off him. Instead, the police arrested the man on the spot, along with another disciple who was in the car with him.

The Mexican police insisted the pair accompany them to Rancho Santa Elena, as they'd already had numerous reports about the Hernández cartel's activities on the property. But when the police arrived with the two suspects, the ranch was deserted. Adolfo and the Hernández brothers had been tipped off about the original arrests by a source inside the police.

Adolfo had taken off with Sara Aldrete, his two long-term male lovers Martín Quintana Rodríguez and Omar Orea Ochoa, and Hernández gang hit man Alvaro de Leon Valdez – known as 'El Duby' to his friends. A preliminary search of the main buildings of the ranch turned up a shipment of marijuana plus several firearms. The two gang members who'd been arrested were taken to a police station to be interrogated. Later that evening, they talked openly with a perverse kind of pride about black magic, torture and even human sacrifice.

Meanwhile, other investigators back at the ranch quizzed the elderly caretaker, who mentioned in passing that he'd met a young American on the premises a few weeks earlier. The description he gave sounded just like missing student Mark Kilroy.

Police then reinterviewed the two men they'd locked up at a local police station. They admitted taking part in Kilroy's abduction and murder, and confessed that the killing was one of many committed over the previous 18 months at Rancho Santa Elena.

The two suspects referred to the slayings, however, as human sacrifices. They insisted the killings had to be carried out to ensure occult 'protection' in relation to numerous drug deals.

'It's our religion,' the Hernández gang member explained to detectives. 'Our voodoo. We have to make sacrifices to protect our produce.'

The following day, the police returned to the ranch with the suspects once again. They identified the ranch's private graveyard behind the main building. Police then uncuffed both men and ordered them to start digging, and warned them they would be shot if they refused. Within minutes, one of them had unearthed what would be the first of 12 bodies found to have been buried in a neat row.

All the victims appeared to be men. Some had been shot at close range, others had clearly been hacked to death with a machete. One of the bodies resembled Mark Kilroy. His skull had been split open and his brain removed.

On entering a nearby shed, investigators found Adolfo's cast-iron nganga kettle, brimming with blood, animal remains and 28 sticks used for Palo Mayombe ceremonies. The men told police the sticks had been used to communicate with spirits in the afterlife. Floating in the pot, along with dead spiders and scorpions, were the remains of Mark Kilroy's brain.

Over the following six days, the butchered bodies of another 15 victims were recovered from the ranch's unofficial cemetery. Three additional corpses were also found buried in a nearby orchard. The majority of victims had either been slashed with knives or shot or both. At least one had been burned to death and another hanged. Most of the bodies had had their hearts, ears, eyes and testicles removed. Some were even decapitated.

When investigators accused their suspects of murdering the people whose remains they'd just dug up, they insisted that a man known only as 'El Padrino' was the only person who'd carried out the actual killings. They claimed he was the mastermind and religious leader behind all the killings, but there was no sign of Adolfo de Jesús Constanzo – still just 26 years of age. Also missing was Sara Aldrete, described to police as Adolfo's *madrina* – godmother. Disciples alleged that she had killed several of the victims alongside Adolfo.

The following day, police raided the house in Matamoros that Sara Aldrete still occasionally shared with her parents. In her bedroom, they uncovered a makeshift altar of black candles, beaded necklaces and cigars hidden behind what appeared to be a blood-splattered wall. There was no sign of Aldrete herself.

Meanwhile detectives reported all the occult elements of the case to their *comandante*. He halted the investigation immediately, insisting the search could not resume until all the black magic items had been properly destroyed, to kill off any of the evil spirits that may be thriving on the ranch.

Two American lawmen present that day tried to convince the *comandante* that it was essential to keep all such evidence for use in an eventual trial. But the officer was adamant that a special purification rite had to be carried out by a *curandero* (healer).

The healer they called in then went through a series of hand motions before closing his eyes and making the sign of the cross. After setting light to the shack, he threw bags of white powder on the flames in order to drive away the evil spirits. Mexican police insisted that by destroying the shack, they'd wiped out Adolfo's power, which would prevent him and his disciples reigniting their occult activities.

A number of informants told Mexican and American investigators that Adolfo would most likely run home to his mother. In fact, Adolfo was in a small apartment on Rio Sena in the centre of Mexico City. With him were Sara Aldrete, his two male lovers Martín Quintana Rodríguez and Omar Orea Ochoa, and Hernández *sicario* El Duby. Adolfo kept an Uzi by his side at all times and rarely slept for more than a few minutes at a time.

On 22 April 1989, Adolfo watched a TV news bulletin about the raid on the ranch which featured footage of his beloved tin shack temple being razed to the ground in the presence of the *curandero*. Adolfo exploded and began smashing up the apartment. He threw lamps on the floor and overturned furniture and then locked himself in the toilet.

On the other side of Mexico City, the police raided Adolfo's empty luxury home in Atizapán where they discovered stockpiles of pornography and a hidden ritual chamber, but no sign of their chief suspect.

On 18 April 1989 – with Adolfo now being publicly referred to as Mexico's most wanted man – he sat round a table in the small apartment with Sara Aldrete, his two male lovers and hit man El Duby and told them his tarot cards were saying that one of them had betrayed him.

Adolfo muttered darkly: 'They (the police) cannot kill you. But I can.'

Sara became so worried she was about to be killed by Adolfo that she hastily scribbled a note on a piece of paper and threw it out from a bedroom window on to the street below.

It read: *'Please call the judicial police and tell them that in this building are those that they are seeking. Tell them that a woman is being held hostage. I beg for this, because what I want most is to talk – or they're going to kill the girl.'*

A passer-by found the note almost immediately, read it, but kept it to themselves, convinced it must have been someone's lame attempt at humour.

Inside the crowded apartment, Adolfo had calmed down enough to relay plans for them all to flee Mexico. 'We'll start our lives somewhere else,' he insisted to them. 'They'll never take me alive.'

On 6 May 1989 – just weeks after Adolfo had watched the burning of his beloved shrine at the ranch – the *Federales* surrounded a rust-coloured apartment building on a quiet residential street in Mexico City after neighbours called police to complain about a loud argument inside one apartment, which had then been accompanied by gunshots.

The police who arrived at the building on Rio Sena began going door-to-door asking questions, unaware that Mexico's most wanted man was living there. They were actually searching for a missing local child and presumed the gunshots were related to that case.

Not knowing the police were in the building, but fearing that the end was near anyway, Adolfo leaned out of the window of the 15th-storey apartment and aimed his Uzi machine gun casually at passers-by without pressing the trigger. Then he began throwing handfuls of banknotes out.

As they fluttered down towards the street below, Adolfo spotted the police from the window ledge. He presumed they'd come to get him and immediately panicked and opened fire with his gun. Within minutes, more than 100 policemen had surrounded the apartment block and were returning fire. Thus began a 45-minute shoot-out which, miraculously, resulted in just one person being wounded, one of the policemen who first answered the call.

Inside the apartment, Adolfo grew so despondent that he hadn't been shot by police that he stopped firing and handed his Uzi to hit man El Duby and ordered him to kill him and his lover Quintana. El Duby later told police: 'I told him I couldn't do it. But then he hit me in the face and threatened me that everything would go bad for me in hell.'

Adolfo told the nervous El Duby to wait while he carefully positioned himself on a stool inside a bedroom closet and beckoned his lover to sit beside him. Adolfo kissed Quintana gently on the lips before turning and nodding to El Duby, who dutifully squeezed the trigger of the machine gun.

After hearing the shots, police stormed the apartment. El Duby, Aldrete and three of Adolfo's other disciples surrendered immediately. The bodies of Adolfo and Rodríguez were found slumped inside the closet, their shirts smeared with blood. Adolfo was dressed in shorts as if he was about to head off for a day at the beach.

In the apartment, the *Federales* also found black candles, two swords, a skull made of white wax and a blindfolded doll holding another doll. El Duby, Orea and Sara Aldrete plus the other disciples were arrested and taken off to jail. They were charged with homicide, criminal association, wounding a police agent and damage to property.

Once in custody, El Duby admitted shooting Adolfo, but warned police: 'The godfather will not be dead for long.'

He insisted that Adolfo would 'rise again', even though his bullet-riddled body lay sprawled on the floor of that bedroom walk-in closet.

Aldrete told police that she didn't see the killings of the people whose bodies were found on the ranch. She claimed she did not know about any of them until she saw news of the killings on television.

She also claimed she'd been kidnapped and kept in another room of the apartment, even insisting she had not seen hit man El Duby shoot Adolfo and his lover dead in the closet.

'It was like hell,' Aldrete told police. 'They treated me like a prisoner.'

Despite her protestations, police were convinced that Aldrete was a willing member of the group and that she'd lured at least some of the victims to their deaths.

While the Godfather's end had already come, police feared that some of Adolfo's other disciples still at large might seek revenge and could well be planning to take his place. Other disciples in custody had also told police that Adolfo's cult extended far beyond Matamoros and into the highest echelons of Mexican society.

* * *

In Matamoros and the surrounding Rio Grande Valley areas, the streets remained eerily quiet for many months following the grisly discovery of those shallow graves on the ranch.

However, town meetings and university seminars about voodoo and witchcraft attracted vast crowds. Attendances at churches also swelled.

Nervous Texans pulled their children out of the school that Sara Aldrete had attended after one former disciple at the Hernández ranch told a local newspaper that satanists inspired by Adolfo were planning to kidnap children in retaliation for the police raid on the ranch.

Funerals were held and death certificates were drawn up, but the ghost of Adolfo de Jesús Constanzo could not yet be completely laid to rest. On 9 May 1989 – two days after that shoot-out outside Adolfo's apartment block in Mexico City – a final bizarre twist in the case emerged.

The *New York Times* suggested in an article that Adolfo's death could have been faked and that he was still at large. Armando Ramírez – resident agent running the United States Drug Enforcement Administration offices across the border in Brownsville – admitted to the newspaper that the faces of Adolfo and Quintana had been so badly mutilated by machine gun bullets that positive identification had not been possible.

Ramírez said the final confirmation of Adolfo's death would have to wait until fingerprints and dental charts could prove beyond doubt it really was Adolfo who'd died in that apartment. Forensic tests did later come back and confirmed

Adolfo really was dead, yet allegations about him being alive still persist to this day.

As the case unfolded, Mexican law enforcement investigators eventually uncovered evidence that several senior police officers had been initiated into Adolfo's religious movement. They alleged that the same officers had hidden away $5.5 million in cash and jewellery, which they'd collected as bribes from drug cartels.

In the end, a total of 14 of Adolfo's disciples were arrested and indicted on various charges, including multiple murder, weapons and narcotics violations, conspiracy and obstruction of justice.

In August 1990, hit man El Duby was convicted of killing Adolfo and his lover Quintana and given a 35-year prison term. Other cultists were convicted of murder and sentenced to 35 years each. Adolfo's lover Omar Orea – convicted in the same case – died of AIDS before he could be sentenced.

In 1990, Sara Aldrete was convicted of criminal association and jailed for six years. In a second trial in 1994, she faced several charges of murder connected to the killings at the ranch.

Experts told the court that Aldrete showed clear signs of having a split personality. In the public glare of TV news lights she seemed charming, but away from the crowds she was tense and short-tempered and in complete denial about her role in so many murders.

And throughout her second trial, when Aldrete was asked repeatedly who killed Mark Kilroy, she repeated over and over again: 'Adolfo.'

Aldrete also insisted to the court that she felt sorry about the murders of Mark Kilroy and the others. 'If I'd known it was like this, I wouldn't have been in it,' she said of the cult.

Jurors didn't believe her plea of innocence, and so Aldrete and four male accomplices were convicted of multiple murders at the ranch. Aldrete was sentenced to 62 years, while other disciples were given prison terms totalling 67 years. American authorities publicly stated they would prosecute Aldrete, El Duby and their disciples for Mark Kilroy's murder, should they ever be released from custody.

From her prison cell, Sara Aldrete told reporters: 'I don't think the religion will end with us, because it has a lot of people in it. It will continue.'

Meanwhile, a long list of other cult-related crimes remained unsolved in Mexico. During the two years between 1987 and 1989, when Adolfo was at the peak of his murderous spree, police in Mexico City alone recorded 74 unsolved ritual murders, 14 of them involving infant victims.

Some investigators were accused of trying to clear every ritualistic murder on the books by posthumously blaming Adolfo. Police in Mexico admit they are uncertain of Adolfo's final body count to this day. Most presume that the full number of his victims will probably never be known and so the ghost of Adolfo Constanzo still looms over the Mexican badlands like an evil god.

CHAPTER SIX

THE SILENT WOMAN
JUANA DAYANARA BARRAZA SAMPERIO

Juana Dayanara Barraza Samperio was born in Epazoyucan, Hidalgo, a mainly rural state north of Mexico City. Her mother Justa was just 13 years old when she gave birth to her daughter on 27 December 1957.

Three months later, schoolgirl Justa walked out on the father of their baby – truck driver Trinidad Barraza – after discovering he'd fathered as many as 32 children with other women. He even admitted he'd lost count of how many offspring he actually had.

Justa was broke so she had no choice but to return to the brothel where she'd met Trinidad in the first place. She kept her baby daughter in a makeshift cot in the same bedroom where she slept with men for money.

Juana herself later recalled that one of her first memories was when she was about two and was woken up by the sound of her mother sobbing. She sat up and watched through the bars of her cot as her mother lay face down in a pillow gasping for air as a balding, fat old man thrust himself into her on the bed next to the child.

Juana cried out for her mother over and over again because she sensed the man was hurting her. He eventually stopped and looked across angrily at the toddler before getting off her mother and moving towards her cot.

Justa pulled the man back and pleaded with him not to go near the child and started fondling him to divert him from hurting her daughter. Juana Barraza later claimed she didn't remember what happened after that. But there is no doubt the child quickly became immune to the disturbing noises and activities occurring every night inside that small, badly painted bedroom above the main bar of the brothel.

There were many occasions when customers hit Juana's mother in front of her. Justa usually tried not to cry out in pain in the hope her daughter wouldn't be woken up after what had happened that first time.

From the age of five, Juana's mother forced her daughter to hide under the bed whenever she had 'customers' in case any of them attacked her. Juana endured the sound of thumping, heavy breathing and squeaking mattress springs while trying to keep completely silent to ensure those men didn't know a child was hiding beneath them. This taught her the value of silence from an early age, a lesson that stayed with her for the rest of her life.

When Juana turned 10, the owner of the brothel suggested to Justa that she could charge men a lot of money to deflower her daughter because many of them wanted sex with virgins. Justa wasn't shocked by the suggestion. She'd been sold for sex herself when she'd been younger than her daughter, so – instead of being protective towards her daughter – desperate Justa agreed to allow men to have sex with Juana.

Juana later recalled her mother had insisted she had no choice in the matter saying she was afraid they'd be thrown out of the brothel and made homeless. However, Justa did at least insist on being in the room whenever men had sex with her daughter, to make sure she was safe.

Juana was never able to express at the time how she felt about what was happening in her life as her mother refused to discuss her feelings about anything. She preferred drowning her sorrows in alcohol and drugs.

After suffering two years of continual sexual abuse at the hands of men who visited the brothel, Juana became almost like a robot. She later recalled that all her emotional responses switched off. She would just lie there, close her eyes and try to imagine a world of happiness. Once again, silence was her main coping mechanism.

One evening, Justa found herself drinking a bottle of beer in the bar of the brothel talking to one of her regular, elderly customers called José Lugo. After he'd bought her a third beer, he lowered his voice to a virtual whisper and proposed that in exchange for the drinks he'd just bought her, he'd like to be given her daughter permanently.

Light-headed from the alcohol, Justa simply shrugged her shoulders and nodded in agreement. She later claimed she genuinely hoped José Lugo would give her daughter a better life than the one they had inside that brothel.

Justa promised Juana that José Lugo would look after her, though she also advised her daughter to move in with the old man, if she wanted to have 'a nice life'. She also advised her daughter to get pregnant as quickly as possible.

A year later, Juana was visiting her mother when she started feeling sick one morning and Justa cheerily announced she must be expecting a child. Juana asked if she could get rid of it.

Justa was appalled by the suggestion and coldly ordered her daughter to continue living with the old man and have the child in the hope he would then support them all. Juana was 13, the exact same age as her mother had been when she had her. But just days after agreeing to her mother's orders, Juana miscarried the baby.

When Justa discovered she'd lost the child, she beat Juana, convinced she'd had an abortion after all. Many years later, it emerged that Justa had actually been promised an extra cash 'bonus' by Lugo if Juana had a baby with him.

Both mother and daughter presumed the old man would end his relationship with Juana after she lost the baby. But instead he took pity on Juana and encouraged her to continue living with him. However, he also made it clear he was hoping she would get pregnant again.

Over the following three years, teenager Juana endured José Lugo's constant sexual demands and he remained as determined as ever she would have his child. Juana burst into tears every time she saw her mother and had to admit she still wasn't pregnant. Justa would then just blandly remind her of her 'obligations' to 'kind' José Lugo.

When Juana finally got pregnant again at the age of 16, she was too afraid to tell anyone about it. But then her mother spotted the tell-tale signs and insisted she tell José Lugo. Within two weeks, she'd miscarried that pregnancy as well.

When José Lugo found out, he kicked Juana out of his home. With nowhere else to live, Juana returned to the brothel where her mother still worked.

Justa was furious with her daughter for losing the child and informed her that God must have deliberately taken the baby away from Juana because she hadn't gone to church enough. Juana pleaded with her mother to let her stay with her at the brothel. Her mother would only agree if her daughter handed over to her all the money she was paid by men to have sex. Justa also insisted that she and her daughter pretend to be sisters when they went to bed with customers in the brothel, so they could earn more money, as the men would think Justa was younger than she really was.

Teenager Juana was so emotionally detached from her life by this time that she struggled to make normal conversation. It was only many years later that she realised that going inside herself emotionally was the only way she could handle what was happening to her at that time.

Juana later recalled how she'd lie on her back, close her eyes tight and think about the two babies she'd lost as man after man climbed on top of her and thrust themselves into her. She imagined her 'lost' children being happy in heaven because it had to be a better place than where she'd ended up.

Juana usually only opened her eyes after the men had finished. Then she'd force herself to smile at them in the hope they'd give her a tip. But she wasn't a good actress and few of the men ever left her one. The fee they'd paid beforehand went straight to her mother who'd then split it with the owner of the brothel.

Juana later said she had sex with an average of at least half a dozen strangers each night and became convinced there was no other life out there beyond the perimeter of the bordello. Meanwhile, Juana's addled, greedy mother Justa continued to waste most of their cash on drugs and alcohol for herself.

By the time Juana reached her early twenties, she had big bags under her eyes and a saggy neck, which made her look at least 10 years older than she was. And her increasingly resentful mother continued to remind her that if she'd had a child with José Lugo, they would have both had a better life. Juana began to believe she'd blown their only chance of ever escaping that brothel and the only way out now was probably in a wooden box.

But her mother's criticism was short-lived because within three or four years of starting work in the brothel, alcoholic drug addict Justa had succumbed to cirrhosis of the liver. Juana said later she felt more relief than sadness about her mother's death. She hoped this might be an opportunity to escape her nightmare of a life.

Over the previous three or four years, Juana had been secretly saving money from clients that she never declared to her mother or the brothel keeper. It wasn't a fortune but she had enough to head to Mexico City to start a new life.

There were, however, many obstacles in Juana's way. She'd had very little education during her childhood and hadn't even learned how to properly read or write. How on earth could she survive in one of the world's biggest cities? But Juana convinced herself that in Mexico City she'd find herself a wealthy man and this time she'd have a baby with him and they would live happily ever after.

The only man she found was both jobless and a drunk, and he expected her to go out and work. She married him but soon discovered that getting pregnant came with no guarantees of a happy life, despite what her mother had always said.

Her husband was also extremely violent towards her. The marriage was a disaster and she ended up alone again but with the added responsibility of raising two children on her own in a tiny, cramped apartment in one of Mexico City's poorest districts.

With no financial help from her ex-husband, Juana tried desperately to find a legitimate way to make money. With many mouths to feed and a determination not to end up working in a brothel, Juana turned to other types of crimes in order to keep her family afloat.

She regularly shoplifted food and clothes from stores near her home. She eventually got arrested and only avoided a prison sentence when the judge took pity on her after she told him she had two young children to feed and no husband.

Back in the crumbling apartment block where she lived, Juana wracked her brains to try and work out how to earn enough money to support her family. She feared that if she didn't act fast then her children could be taken away from her by social services.

Stuck at home day and night, Juana became hooked on watching TV and alternated between cheesy soap operas and lucha libre, a form of Mexican masked professional wrestling in which the wrestlers engaged in titanic mock battles. Wrestling was (and still is) one of the biggest spectator sports in Mexico.

Juana would spend hours glued to her TV set even late at night while her children were asleep. She avidly studied all the moves and tried to predict who was going to win.

She then discovered that one of her neighbours was a retired female wrestler on the local lucha libre circuit, which was immensely popular at the time. While discussing the world of wrestling with her neighbour, Juana realised that wrestling might make an ideal outlet for all her anger, which often boiled over when she was dealing with her children.

Juana attended a local, free gym to get fit enough to start wrestling. Then – with no experience of fighting – she persuaded the neighbour to help train her.

She told Juana that she needed to develop her own unique wrestling persona in order to stand any chance of making it as a professional wrestler.

Enter *La Dama del Silencio*.

Her name in English meant 'The Silent Lady' and it was a very apt description for Juana, whose brutal childhood had left her quiet and reserved and unable to show any emotion, apart from an occasional grimace.

Juana's stern demeanour made her appear extremely scary, which was important when trying to appeal to the sport's predominantly male audience. Juana had no plans to titillate the audience like most other female wrestlers, though. She saw herself as a 'madre' (mother figure) of the ring.

La Dama del Silencio's wrestling wardrobe consisted of a butterfly mask, T-shirt and striped pink leggings under baggy shorts. When she was introduced to the audience at her very first bout, commentators and male audience members mocked the frizzy orange ponytail sticking out of the back of her mask because it made her look as if she'd been electrocuted just before entering the ring.

When the fight promoter at that first bout insisted Juana should wear tight satin hot pants, she stormed out of the dressing room and refused to fight. She only changed her mind when the promoter apologised for his sexist comments.

This tough, no-nonsense approach actually helped Juana's career at the start because it stood her apart from many other female wrestlers on the circuit at the time who liked to project themselves as 'sex bombs' in the belief that it would help them win over audiences.

But Juana's reputation wasn't helped when the crowd got a brief glimpse of Barraza's granite-like face beneath her butterfly mask after an opponent unsportingly ripped it off. The crowd laughed at La Dama del Silencio's humiliation as she grappled on the canvas trying to retrieve her mask.

After that incident, some male audience members started comparing Juana to their elderly mothers. Others made homophobic comments about La Dama del Silencio's sexuality, as she seemed very masculine compared to many of the other fighters.

Beneath her butterfly mask, she hid a simmering resentment for most people, and this was further fuelled by all the nasty jibes from those cruel, insensitive male audience members. While people would speculate about her, none of her female opponents and promoters bothered to ask Juana Dayanara Barraza Samperio who she really was or why she'd decided to become a wrestler.

Juana later explained that she chose the name La Dama del Silencio 'because I was and still am quiet and keep myself to myself'. And that silence was useful when she became pregnant by a new husband during those early days of her wrestling career. Afraid they'd stop her fighting – and then she wouldn't be able to feed her kids – she said nothing and kept on wrestling.

La Dama del Silencio's first half-dozen fights ended in crushing defeats, though, and she was warned by promoters that if she didn't start winning soon then she'd be kicked off the women's wrestling circuit.

Juana then had to pretend to be injured so that she could have her latest child. She returned to the ring just two weeks after giving birth and even managed three straight victories over the following two-month period on her local women's wrestling circuit. Juana began to find herself more appreciated by the audience, who now accepted her as an archetypal wrestling 'baddy'. This made her perfect fodder for fight promoters, who planned to start putting her up against some of the big-hitting so-called glamour queens of the circuit.

Throughout this period, Juana continued training very hard. She'd put her children to bed at night and then slip out of the apartment and head for a nearby gym where no one even realised she was the notorious La Dama del Silencio. But the predominantly male audiences who packed wrestling venues throughout the city continued to dismiss La Dama del Silencio as an 'ugly old witch' when she went on another losing run.

No one inside Mexico City's tightly knit wrestling community knew much about Juana because she kept to herself and usually rushed off back to her family as soon as her fight was over, and so she knew only too well that nobody really cared whether Juana lost or won.

La Dama del Silencio continued to only ever get minor billing in the small print at the bottom of most fight cards, if her name was even mentioned in the first place. Often, she was a last-minute replacement, which meant no one in the audience even knew she was on the bill until she was introduced by the referee during the noisy fight prelims.

La Dama del Silencio would then spend the majority of each bout bouncing back and forth off the ropes before ending up on the canvas floor with a heavy thud as the audience jeered enthusiastically. Most fights did not need to be rigged as wrestlers like Juana were deliberately chosen because they were so clearly 'inferior' to their opponents. Her sneering, often theatrical opponents would then stand over her, hands on hips, smirking down at her as the crowd urged them on to finish her off.

Being a punchbag for her opponents wasn't exactly good for Juana's health. She'd often hobble back into the family's tiny apartment covered in bruises after yet another defeat in the ring. While these injuries always seemed tough, within a few days Juana would be back in the ring on the receiving end of yet another battering. She needed the money, even though it was never more than a couple of hundred dollars per fight.

As her injuries piled up, even the most hardened fight promoters began refusing to put La Dama del Silencio on their bill due to her poor physical condition. On those occasions, she'd end up selling popcorn in the audience, if she was lucky.

Juana was in a state of complete and utter emotional confusion. She was desperate to continue wrestling because it was her main source of income. She also had to contend with her latest lazy husband who'd lost his job months earlier.

In the middle of all this, Juana became pregnant again by that latest husband. And as she'd done previously, she kept her pregnancy secret and continued fighting on the wrestling circuit.

Not surprisingly, Juana's career in wrestling was fading fast. Promoters were paying her lower fees and she was reluctant to properly take on her opponents much of the time because of her pregnancy. She was also increasingly reluctant to leave her three other children alone at night while she was out wrestling. So just a few weeks after enduring the difficult birth of her fourth child, Juana decided to return to shoplifting again, as it seemed an easier option than the wrestling ring.

Juana's shoplifting skills were pretty rusty by this time and she had two extremely close shaves while stealing from a local supermarket, both of which almost got her arrested. After these near misses, Juana concluded it would be a lot easier to target people's homes for burglaries during the daytime while they were out at work.

The first couple of break-ins proved easy for her and she even found it relatively simple to sell the jewellery and other valuables she stole on the black market in the barrio. And it was certainly much more profitable than shoplifting.

But on her third job, Juana broke into a house that was occupied and was almost caught when the owner shot at her as she fled through the backyard empty-handed. Realising this path was perhaps a little too dangerous, she decided to stop.

A few weeks later, and still without a solid income, Juana got talking to a woman she'd met in the neighbourhood who was a single mother. They were both broke and needed a criminal enterprise that would guarantee them decent money. They decided that both of them could dress up as nurses and rob elderly people living alone during the daytime. That way they wouldn't be risking their own safety because their victims wouldn't even know they'd been robbed, until after they'd left the premises.

Over the following couple of years, Juana and her accomplice successfully robbed more than a dozen homes. Overworked and underpaid local police made little effort to track down the criminals involved because they were already swamped with murders, rapes and other more serious barrio crimes.

On 25 November 2002, Juana and her accomplice talked their way into the home of 64-year-old widow María de la Luz

González Anaya. But within minutes, María was confront-
ing the two women and accusing them of being liars. When
neither Juana nor her accomplice reacted, the elderly lady
became even more agitated and grabbed her telephone, threatening to call the police.

Juana and her associate glanced at each other and nodded,
albeit reluctantly. They'd discussed this moment many times
before but had never had to face the consequences of their
crimes until now.

Juana picked up a large vase and smashed it over María
de la Luz González's head. She fell down unconscious on the
floor. But when she began stirring, Juana sighed and knelt
down next her. Then, looking up at her partner in crime, she
shrugged her shoulders before placing both hands around the
old lady's neck and began squeezing tightly. The old lady's eyes
snapped open wide for a few moments before slowly shutting
again while Juana gritted her teeth as she carried on choking
the life out of her victim.

After González's body had finally gone limp, both women
positioned her corpse on her couch by sitting it up, although
her head was slumped at a strange angle to one side. The two
women believed they'd made it look as if she'd died naturally.
Neither of them thought about the fingermarks on her neck,
which clearly showed she'd been strangled.

Juana later claimed she'd been on such an adrenaline 'high'
at the time that she didn't think much about the death of the

old lady, even after they'd left the apartment. She had learned many times as a child how to cut off from everything, and so a certain emotional detachment came quite easily.

Luckily for them, no witnesses had seen the two 'nurses' entering or leaving their victim's home. It seemed unlikely the police would even manage to work out how or why María de la Luz González had died.

As Juana later recalled: 'It dawned on both of us then that maybe killing them was actually safer for us.'

Juana and her partner in crime lay low for a couple of days as a safety precaution, just in case the police did come looking for them. When that didn't happen and there were no reports in the local newspaper, the two women decided to continue their crime spree.

On 2 March 2003, the two women dressed up as nurses again and talked their way into the home of 84-year-old widow Guillermina León Oropeza. Unable to find any of her valuables while the old lady was in the kitchen making them a cup of coffee, the pair eventually tied her up and tortured her until she told them where everything was.

Having collected each item and placed them in a bag they'd brought with them, the two women stood over the terrified old lady lying tied up on the floor in front of them and stared down at her for a few moments. Then with a casual nod to each other, Juana lent down and put her hands around the old lady's neck and began squeezing so hard her knuckles went white. She later admitted it was much easier each time they carried out a killing and they left the house shortly afterwards, convinced that, once again, they'd got away with murder.

Juana also later confessed that after each new victim, she felt less guilt than she had for the previous killing. Both women believed it was the perfect way to make sure they didn't get caught.

But there was another even more disturbing force driving Juana to kill, that she wasn't disclosing to her partner in crime. Her elderly women victims were of a similar age to Juana's mother if she'd lived long enough. And, as she squeezed the life out of them, Juana convinced herself each victim was her mother. She later admitted this made it easier to kill them.

Over the remainder of 2003, the two women broke into at least five more homes occupied by old ladies living alone and Juana murdered them all. Their last victim that year was Alicia Cota Ducoin, just one month before Christmas.

Despite obvious similarities, the hard-pressed local police had yet to link the murders to each other. It was also clear to the victim's relatives that the murders of old people were not high on the police's list of priorities.

Forensic investigators who examined the murder scenes during 2003 began to note that the attacks all shared the same level of violence and brutality. They even suspected that the killings had some personal motivation because the perpetrator seemed so angry towards the victims.

As one officer later recalled: 'The killings were done with venom. Almost as if the killer was doing it out of some sense of revenge. Yet there was no clear evidence of a direct connection between any of the victims and one specific killer.'

Then at the beginning of 2004, La Dama del Silencio decided to try and resurrect her fading wrestling career on Mexico City's female fight circuit. Juana later said the reason for wanting to move back into wrestling was that she wanted to try and stop the killings, even though she wasn't sure she really could.

Back inside the wrestling ring she was lacking the 'killer instinct' to completely finish off opponents. All of them would always then come back at her and give her a terrible battering, which resulted in every single bout being stopped.

Psychoanalysts later connected Juana's lack of success inside the ring directly to her murder spree. One explained: 'All those elderly women were weak and incapable of fighting back. I think Juana looked on them as opponents whom she could actually beat into submission, unlike most of the wrestlers she came across in the ring.'

Each time Juana suffered yet another beating, she found the only way to overcome those failures was to dominate and kill yet another old lady.

In 2004 – the year after Juana's murder spree first began – she killed a total of 15 more elderly women. This included a 70-year-old called María Dolores Martínez Benavides, who was strangled with a stethoscope so violently that her neck was snapped. Forensics who attended the scene noted this as clear evidence of the killer's anger.

The police still had no suspects and officers insisted to the media that none of the evidence they'd collected from crime scenes contained any concrete clues about the identity of the killer and they still struggled with the notion that a serial killer – one person – might be responsible.

Police insisted they were hunting for at least two professional male criminals. They also didn't once consider that a woman could have been responsible for the brutal murders.

In early 2005, 92-year-old María de los Ángeles Repper Hernández was strangled with her own scarf after being beaten to a pulp. Apparently she refused to tell Juana and her accomplice where her jewellery was hidden.

It was only after María's murder that police investigators finally concluded that the killer had talked their way into these old ladies' homes by pretending to be a helper, but it did little to help narrow their search.

One criminologist then publicly announced that because three of the victims owned a print of a painting by the eighteenth-century French artist Jean-Baptiste Greuze (*Boy In A Red Waistcoat*) the murders were connected through art. This gave the clear impression police were hunting a sophisticated, highly intelligent serial killer, who would undoubtedly prove very hard to catch.

Mexico City's chief prosecutor Bernardo Bátiz even announced to the media: 'We're dealing with a brilliant mind!'

Bátiz also claimed that the serial killer in their midst was so super intelligent that he'd been 'extra careful' not to leave any clues which had made the police's job even harder. The media in Mexico City interpreted this as a lame excuse for a poorly managed police investigation.

Then two eyewitnesses came forward and provided police with enough information for them to issue a sketch of an alleged *Mataviejita* – 'Old Lady Killer' – as the newspaper called the perpetrator. Detectives insisted the image they'd produced was of a man dressed as a woman. When challenged, the police said they believed the suspect was most likely a transvestite.

A police press release issued at the time stated: 'The killer is a man, dressed as a woman in white, height between 1.7 and 1.75 metres [basically around 5 feet 6 inches], robust complexion, light brown, oval face, wide cheeks, blond hair, delineated eyebrows and approximately 45 years old.'

In fact, the witnesses who'd come forward had helped police construct a photofit that looked remarkably like Juana, right down to the close-cropped hair dyed blonde and a facial mole. This latest description was accompanied by a detailed psychological profile, which inexplicably referred to previous male serial killers who had targeted elderly women in Europe.

The police even highlighted one killer called Thierry Paulin – better known as the 'Beast of Montmartre' – who between

1984 and 1987 had murdered at least 25 elderly women in France. The police statements had a detrimental effect on the overall investigation because they seemed to ignore clear evidence that there were in fact two suspects, and also that they were both women.

The next profile released by the police stated: 'The killer is a man with homosexual preferences, and a victim of childhood physical abuse. He could have had a grandmother or lived with an elderly person, and has resentment to that feminine figure and possesses great intelligence.'

When the press dared to speculate that the mass killer was most likely female and that she had an accomplice, the police pointed out that only a few years earlier – in 1998 – highly respected FBI profilers had insisted 'there are no female serial killers'.

Back in the barrio, Juana struggled to manage her three completely separate lives as a mother of four children struggling to make ends meet, a fast-fading female wrestler La Dama del Silencio and a serial killer. Then two of those bizarre worlds collided when her 24-year-old street gangster eldest son was killed after being attacked with a baseball bat (some said he was shot) during a skirmish between rival criminals in Mexico City.

Juana later claimed that her son's murder made her want to punish the world because of everything that had happened to him and her. But all this very conveniently ignored the fact that she'd already killed more than 20 innocent elderly women with her own hands before her son died.

Juana became so immersed in grief that her second oldest child – a girl in her late teens – left home and married just after her brother's murder. But she stayed close enough to Juana's small first-floor apartment for help bringing up her two younger children.

Meanwhile, Mexico City police's much-criticised investigation into the serial killings petered out once again when Juana stopped her killings for much of 2005 after falling out with her accomplice. Relatives of many victims once again accused detectives of still not trying hard enough because their loved ones were so elderly. Some police officers even privately admitted the killer would have to strike again in order to provide them with more clues if they were going to stand any chance of catching the killer.

In October 2005, Mexico City homicide investigators announced to reporters that they believed the killer had committed suicide, as no one had been murdered that entire year.

To prove their claim, the police took random fingerprints found at the six most recent murder scenes and cross-referenced them with the fingerprints of recent Mexico City suicide victims. But when this failed to come up with any matches, police investigators switched their attention back to Mexico City's transgender community, following those earlier claims that the killers wore women's clothing.

Police went on to interrogate a total of 49 of the city's transsexuals and transvestites. Afterwards, many of these so-called suspects alleged the police had used brutality and torture to try and get them to confess to crimes they hadn't committed. After failing to find the perpetrator this way, and struggling to think of their next move in the investigation, detectives finally concluded that their killer could well be a woman after all.

When Juana read all this in one of the city's newspapers, she felt quite exhilarated that investigators seemed to have finally worked out the sex of the killer. Then, in a bizarre act of defiance, she decided it was time to head out to find another victim.

Juana was convinced the inept police were so far from solving the case that she might as well kill again while she could still get away with it. She also needed some money. Juana's earlier accomplice was no longer involved but that made no real difference because Juana had always been the one who did the actual killing anyway.

In November 2005, Juana targeted 82-year-old Carmen Camila González Miguel at her apartment. After talking her way into the old lady's home, she tied her up and forced her to lie on the floor and then demanded that Carmen tell her where all her most valuable possessions were.

When the old lady refused to tell Juana, she strangled her. But she later admitted it didn't feel the same as it had when she'd murdered all her previous victims. This time, Juana was left feeling nervous and vulnerable by her own actions. She even started to question her own mental health for the first time. Why was she doing this? Had she changed as a person during the long gap between this and her previous killings?

Also, Juana's latest victim Carmen turned out to be the mother of respected Mexican criminologist Luis Rafael Moreno González. He immediately demanded police action so the *Federales* announced the launch of *Operación Parques y Jardines* (Operation Parks and Gardens) to try and track down the serial killer in their midst.

Police patrols were quickly stepped up in the areas of Mexico City where the killer had struck. Thousands of flyers were distributed warning of so-called 'stranger danger'. Police even recruited several elderly women to act as 'bait' in those same city areas, while teams of undercover officers hid close by in case the killer approached the old ladies. But despite this sharp increase in police activity, the killer was nowhere to be found.

And in the middle of all this, Juana – as La Dama del Silencio – made a bizarre appearance on a Mexican TV documentary about female wrestlers. She told an interviewer about her life in the sport as the notorious 'Silent Lady'. Juana explained that the character she played in the ring was definitely 'bad to the core'. Many of those watching the programme later said she didn't sound very convincing and her flat, monotone accent seemed totally disconnected from her fearsome wrestling persona.

Juana later recalled that the TV interview irritated her immensely because she had done it without wearing her mask. That made her feel vulnerable and exposed. It also made her look like a publicity seeker. And while the serial killer the police were supposedly hunting appeared on TV watched by millions, the much-heralded *Operación Parques y Jardines* continued to get precisely nowhere.

Back at home, Juana recognised that the murder of her latest victim Carmen might turn out to have been a mistake because her son had galvanised the investigation. So Juana retreated back into her domestic life as the mother of two young children and tried her hardest not to be tempted into committing any more murders. But as the weeks turned into months, she once again found herself struggling to afford to live. She later claimed that in the end, she had no choice but to go out and find another victim.

Three months after the death of elderly Carmen Camila González Miguel, a woman matching one of the latest police descriptions of the serial killer was seen running away from an apartment close to the area where Juana lived.

The witness had been a tenant who rented a room in the home of 84-year-old Ana María de los Reyes Alfaro. She saw Juana hurrying down a corridor towards the entrance lobby of the apartment block. Moments afterwards, the tenant entered the flat to find her elderly landlady dead on the floor. When the police arrived at the scene minutes later, she told officers that the person she saw leaving the flat was definitely a woman and gave them a detailed description of the perpetrator. Mexico City police patrol cars immediately began scouring the area. Investigators now had a reliable witness, who'd hopefully be able to positively identify the woman she saw fleeing from the apartment.

Meanwhile Juana was wandering around the streets near her victim's home in a daze. Not only had she seen the witness as she fled the scene, but she didn't feel empowered like she had after those earlier killings. When Juana heard police sirens in the distance, she had no doubt they were connected to the murder she'd just committed. But she made no attempt to hide or run. She just carried on walking in the direction of her apartment.

Less than an hour later, officers in a patrol car spotted a woman who perfectly matched the tenant's detailed description. They pulled up alongside Juana in a crowded street just a quarter of a mile from her home and drew their guns.

Juana shrugged her shoulders as the two uniform cops ordered her to stand against a wall while they frisked her for weapons and found the stethoscope she'd just used to strangle her latest victim. She also had on her state pension forms and a social worker identification card, which they soon deduced she'd used to talk her way into the old lady's apartment.

Juana even helpfully put her own hands behind her back so they could handcuff her before she was taken in a patrol car to a local police station, where officers obtained a search warrant for her home. There, investigators discovered a cupboard full of trophies stolen from Juana's victims. These included family snapshots and even cutlery. Next to them were boxes containing newspaper clippings of many of the killings she had committed.

While being interrogated back at the police station, Juana admitted to detectives that she'd talked her way into her last victim's apartment by claiming she was seeking work doing laundry. When Juana asked one of the detectives why there were so many journalists and TV cameras outside the police station, the officer said they were all there for her. She blushed.

'For me?' she asked.

'Yep, you're the first woman serial killer we've had around these parts,' replied the detective.

However Juana wasn't prepared to face up to the full responsibility of being a mass murderer so she told police: 'I only killed one little old lady. Not the others.'

A few minutes later, police escorted Juana in handcuffs out of the front of the police station towards a van waiting to take her to prison for the night. She was greeted with a barrage of bright lights and the buzz of camera motor drives as one journalist shouted at her: 'Are you a serial killer, señora?'

Juana smiled into the bright camera lights and said: 'Yes, I did it.'

But then she stopped for a moment as she thought about what she'd just said and then added: 'Just because I'm going to pay for it, doesn't mean they're going to hang all the crimes on me.'

When another reporter asked Juana about the stethoscope and the fake paperwork she'd had on her when she was arrested, she added: 'That's a lie. I wasn't carrying the documents they have there.'

Juana steadfastly refused to provide a motive to the reporters at the time, but she did tell also them: 'You'll know why I did it when you read my statement to police.'

But when one female journalist asked Juana to explain her motives, she smiled and yelled back: 'I got angry.'

By the following morning, the case was on the front page of all Mexico City's main newspapers. They pointed out to their readers that Juana closely resembled the police's original composite profiles of the 'transvestite' right down to the distinct mole on her face.

Mexico City police told journalists in off-the-record briefings following Juana's arrest that she'd 'more or less' admitted to killing three other women, in addition to final victim Ana María. Detectives also announced that they expected to find Juana's fingerprints at the scene of at least 10 other murders of old ladies in the city, plus a print in the apartment of one of her early victims who survived.

On the morning of 25 January 2006, Juana was officially charged with killing between 42 and 48 elderly women. The media dubbed her Mexico's first ever solo female serial killer.

There was no mention of her alleged accomplice in many of the murders.

At Juana's first court appearance later that same day, she insisted on telling the judge: 'It isn't right to pin the others on me.'

Juana had clearly decided she should deny all involvement in the other killings, apart from most recent victim Ana María and the three other women where her fingerprints had so far been found. Prosecutors, however, insisted to the court that they had clear and irrefutable evidence that Juana was responsible for at least 40 other deaths, despite her denials.

For the following two years, police and prosecutors meticulously collected statements from witnesses, analysed crime scenes and uncovered additional evidence connected to Juana's numerous killings until they were confident they could pursue her in court for all the murders they believed she'd committed.

On 31 March 2008, Juana was found guilty on 16 charges of murder and aggravated burglary, including 11 separate counts of murder. She was sentenced to 759 years in prison.

After receiving her sentence from the judge, Juana told the court: 'May God forgive you and not forget me.'

Sentences imposed in Mexican courts are served concurrently, so the maximum Juana would serve under Mexican law was 60 years. That meant she wouldn't be eligible for parole until 2058, by which time she'd be more than 100 years old.

But serving her sentence in Mexico City's Santa Martha Acatitla prison didn't turn out to be as much of a hardship for Juana as many had expected. She was greeted by most other women inmates as a heroine. They squarely blamed her crimes on the abuse she'd received at the hands of men throughout her life.

Juana spent a lot of her time in prison selling her tasty home-cooked meals to other inmates. Her speciality was *cochinita pibil*, a slow-roasted, spicy pork dish that was Yucatan in origin.

Following the non-stop media coverage of her crimes, Juana's name carried considerable currency within Mexican pop culture. Cumbia pop star Amandititita – who'd once appeared on the same TV wrestling show *Lucha Underground* as Juana – even wrote a hit song about her after hearing it was the serial killer's favourite programme.

'La Mataviejitas wants to get rid of your grandmother,' Amandititita sang to her fans over a loud fusion of rock, reggae and rap. *'No one can stop this shameless person, she is a professional wrestler, she used to call herself La Dama del Silencio. No one suspected or could have imagined such a thing. This killer could be your neighbour ...'*

As well as winning over inmates with her tasty home cooking, Juana also married 74-year-old Miguel Ángel, an inmate in the men's section of the Santa Martha Acatitla prison. He was serving a life sentence for murder.

Ángel had been writing secretly to Juana for more than a year following her trial and they'd exchanged many letters. While they had spoken many times, they didn't actually meet in person until the day of their wedding ceremony, which was held in the prison's canteen.

Juana and Ángel ended up seeing each other for a total of just two hours during three separate visits over the following year before the marriage was dissolved when Juana announced that it was 'meaningless'.

Ángel later said his killer bride spoke very little during their get-togethers and he felt she never properly connected with him. But he did concede that after the life she'd led, he wasn't surprised she never opened up to anyone.

'Silence was Juana's defence against everything that had happened to her,' one detective explained. 'She hoped that if she kept quiet then all her troubles might go away.'

CHAPTER SEVEN

THE CANNIBAL POET
JOSÉ LUIS CALVA ZEPEDA

José Luis Calva Zepeda's siblings always looked the other way when their mother Elia targeted her four-year-old son for a beating. He was the weak one who irritated her and reminded her of her dead husband. His brothers and sisters would shrug their shoulders and head out of their shanty home as their mother's blows began raining down on her shy little child.

José Luis's entire family noticed that from a very young age he seemed different from the other kids in the dusty, tin shack barrio where they all lived in one of the poorest areas of Hidalgo, north of Mexico City. José Luis never knew his father, who died just two years after he was born on 20 June 1969, so there was no man in the household for him to look up to. Most people back then presumed that if a boy grew up without a father figure to guide him through his childhood, then he was more than likely to go astray.

Young José Luis handled his isolation and lack of paren-tal guidance by retreating into his own imagination most of the time. He later recalled that he stepped into a 'distant zone' inside his head whenever his mother began hitting him. And when the pain got too much to bear, he'd snap out of that mindset, wriggle free from her grasp, run as far away from her as possible and usually collapse in floods of tears in an unkempt corner of the family home, where none of his siblings could see or hear him sobbing.

José Luis grew up to loathe his mother. Her tirades of violence and retribution could be sparked by anything from not finishing a meal to being late for bath time. And as he grew older, she'd beat him even harder, especially if he glared at her in a sign of defiance.

José Luis later recalled that he hated living at home so much that he'd often slip out of the family house as soon as his mother fell asleep and spend the night in the backyard under a bush curled up next to the family's mongrel dog. The animal made him feel a lot safer and even provided the boy with some warmth on chilly evenings.

Weekends and public holidays were the worst because his mother Elia would be in the house all day. Not even Christmas time could soften her attitude towards him.

When José Luis was just six years old, he watched through a crack in a door as his mother and eldest sister wrapped gifts for a Mexican post-Christmas children's holiday known as the Three Wise Men. But when Elia Zepeda realised her son was spying on them, she ripped open the door and dragged him by the ear into the room in a fury. She yelled at him that the gifts were supposed to be a surprise for him and his other brothers and sisters and accused him of deliberately ruining this entire process.

José Luis later recalled that his sister looked away as Elia then smacked her son so hard that he fell back and hit his head on the corner of a table. The wound immediately began gushing with blood. Instead of helping him, though, his mother glared down at him with her arms folded, not even bothering to examine the gaping wound.

When José Luis looked up at his mother and grimaced with pain, she grabbed a toy truck that she'd been about to wrap off the same table, threw it on the floor next to him and then crushed it into tiny pieces under the heel of her shoe. The boy did not dare move in case she kicked him. He later recalled that he'd wished at that very moment he had a father, because he might have smashed her in the face for hurting their son.

When young José Luis tried to scramble awkwardly to his feet, his mother pushed him back down at least three times until he managed to wriggle out from her grasp and ran straight out of the house with his mother yelling at him to come back. As José Luis dashed through the dusty yard, he never once slowed down or looked behind him in fear that she might catch him and hurt him again.

The boy ran out on to the busy street, narrowly avoiding a passing car before ducking down an alleyway and sprinting past comatose junkies and beggars slumped against crumbling walls. José Luis was more than half a mile from his family home before he dared slow down. He wasn't sure exactly where he was, but at least he couldn't see or hear his mother behind him.

José Luis – just six years of age – was all alone in the middle of a bustling town centre with nowhere to go and no means to even buy himself a drink or a sandwich. He later said he was so determined not to go home that day that he walked the streets for hours. At least he wasn't being smashed to pieces by her.

José Luis recalled how he kept thinking back to how just a few minutes earlier he'd been so excited by the sight of that toy truck. 'Why had such joy turned to violence?' he later said. 'Why did I feel as if I deserved it?'

All these questions were going through José Luis's head as he passed a toy shop on the edge of a busy shopping arcade. Out of the corner of his eye, he suddenly spotted an almost identical toy truck to the one in his home in the window.

José Luis stopped and pressed his face up against the glass while staring in at the toy. He kept wishing he had the truck and then the pain he'd suffered at the hands of his mother might have all been worth it.

With his face still pressed up against the shop window, an elderly man stopped alongside him to see what the boy was looking at. They got talking and the old man suggested that if José Luis cleaned his shoes for him, then he'd pay him enough to put towards buying that truck.

José Luis looked up at the old man standing next to him and made a split-second judgement. He seemed a genuinely nice person, so José Luis leaned down and ripped off each of the raggedy turn-ups on his trousers and turned them into two makeshift cloths.

Minutes later, the old man sat on a low wall while José Luis knelt down and spat into one piece of that cloth and began buffing up the old man's brown leather shoes. Eventually they were so shiny they sparkled magically in the late afternoon sunlight.

The old man smiled after José Luis had finished before surprising him even further by proving to be as good as his word and actually paying him. José Luis couldn't recall his own mother ever smiling at him and he certainly wasn't used to adults being generous to him either.

Newly emboldened by the old man's generosity, José Luis cleaned half a dozen more men's shoes that afternoon before racing back to the toy shop where he'd earlier seen that truck in the window. But he arrived just as the owner was pulling down the shutters. He ignored the little boy's pleas to stay open and sternly announced he was closed for the day. José Luis kicked the shutters with such blind fury that the shop owner told him he'd call the police if he didn't stop.

All the happiness José Luis had felt just a few minutes earlier had disappeared into thin air. He was back to square one and everyone from his mother to that shopkeeper felt like his enemy.

So with his eyes narrowing, José Luis turned and stomped across the street from the toy shop. He stopped at the entrance to an alleyway and stood watching the man locking the shutters.

When the shopkeeper had left, José Luis ducked down another alleyway that ran behind the toy shop and eventually reached a back door. Using a rock, he smashed at the padlock until it fell off. Then he stepped carefully into the darkened store and looked around until he found the toy truck on a shelf.

After taking it, he stopped momentarily in the middle of the store as he remembered the shopkeeper shouting at him to go away just a few minutes earlier. The man's yelling overlapped into the noise of José Luis's own mother screaming at him earlier that same day. As those two adult voices rang in his head, José Luis grabbed a baseball bat from a shelf and started smashing at all the other toys, over and over again.

José Luis's anger only subsided when he heard the sound of a siren in the distance and presumed someone had called the police. He threw down the baseball bat and darted through the store clutching the toy truck in his hand.

As José Luis emerged into the alleyway behind the shop, he later recalled he felt much less scared about facing his mother. It must have been because he'd just done something entirely for himself. He'd proved that he could survive in the world without her, if he had to.

So José Luis headed back home that evening without any fear for the first time in his life. He even had enough confidence to consider a long-term plan which nobody would be able to stop him doing.

As he climbed the steps up to his home, the front door flew open and his mother stared at him with her arms folded and a face like thunder. She looked down at the toy truck clutched in his hand before smacking him across the face so hard that he fell back down the steps. She then walked down to where he was lying and kicked him in the groin.

But this time José Luis felt no pain. Instead, he curled himself up in a tight ball as she carried on kicking him over and over again. All he cared about was the toy truck lying next to him. But when he tried to reach out for it, she stamped on his arm. Then she stopped, leaned down and snatched the toy off the ground.

'Where did you get this? Did you steal it?' she said accusingly, with the heel of one shoe pressing into his chest as she looked down at him.

Six-year-old José Luis shook his head and breathlessly tried to explain that he'd earned the money to buy it by polishing shoes. But she wasn't listening. She glared down at her son with narrowing eyes for a few moments, as she'd so often done in the past.

'Don't move,' she said.

Then she took her heel off his chest and casually dropped the toy on to the ground next to where he lay. Looking down at him again, she crushed it under her foot just like she'd done with that other toy truck only a few hours earlier.

José Luis later recalled that by this time he felt too traumatised to even cry. After she'd done it, he watched her climbing the wooden steps to the house while he lay on the ground still clutching his stomach. He didn't move until he heard the front door slam behind her.

* * *

Less than a year after the incident with the toy truck, José Luis was raped by a man his mother had invited to stay in their house. José Luis never fully explained what happened to him but later in life he said he thought the man was less to blame than his mother because she'd allowed him in the house in the first place.

That sexual assault resulted in José Luis's simmering rage turning into open warfare towards most adults, especially his mother. José Luis's mother never once stopped to consider why her son was so angry. Instead, she carried on hitting and insulting him every day, unaware that the latest man in her life had raped her own son.

By the time he reached the age of nine or ten, José Luis was frequently staying out late at night to try and avoid further physical and sexual attacks inside the family home. He later claimed he often slept rough in darkened alleyways and on stinking landfill sites, where he would scavenge for food.

During yet another fight with his mother when José Luis was 12, he hit her so hard she had to get medical treatment. Everyone else in José Luis's family knew he wasn't to blame, although no one dared tell his mother this.

She was so angry about her injuries that she ordered José Luis to leave home. He later recalled he couldn't wait to get away from her. 'Anywhere was better than staying at home. I didn't care where I ended up,' he said.

Initially, José Luis's older sister and her husband took pity on him and allowed him to stay at their home nearby. His brother-in-law was a professional magician and he encouraged the teenager to work alongside him as a clown at children's parties.

José Luis later described this as probably the happiest period of his life. Pretending to be a clown gave him a way of expressing his inner self that had been repressed for so much of his childhood, thanks to the fear and trepidation he felt about his mother. For the first time in his short life, José Luis found himself with the freedom to be his own person and he was living among people who didn't want to hit and insult him all the time.

At his sister's home, José Luis immersed himself in reading poetry and books. He later said he found it helped him to escape all the painful memories of his childhood. But he was never far away from pressing his own self-destruct button.

To try and deal with all the emotional turmoil he'd been through, José Luis began drinking heavily. His brother-in-law and sister started noticing that he'd disappear for days at a time on drinking binges.

They appreciated a lot of the reasons behind José Luis's destructive behaviour so felt they didn't have the right to reprimand him about his drinking. José Luis later claimed that drinking was his way of crying out for help, only to discover 'no one was listening'. He wasted virtually all the cash he earned on alcohol.

Still only in his mid-teens, José Luis was consuming an entire bottle of cheap tequila as well as vast amounts of beer each night. All this heavy alcohol consumption warped José Luis's mind to such an extent that he began having twisted nightmares, which were undeniably connected to those disturbing childhood experiences. But instead of being the victim, he was the perpetrator lashing out at everyone around him.

He tried to cope with this by reinventing a different, happy childhood for himself whenever he was talking to anyone new in his life. In order to embellish these lies, though, he ended up drinking even more heavily.

Despite all this inner turmoil, José Luis continued working as a children's clown. 'He always seemed happiest when he was playing the clown,' his brother-in-law later recalled. 'It was as if he could hide behind the face paint and relate to all the kids in a way no one ever related to him when he was young.'

Recalling those days, José Luis explained that pretending to be a clown came at a cost, because after he removed the face paint he found himself even more unable to face the harsh realities of his disturbing past. José Luis knew only too well that being a clown was just a form of avoidance. He needed another person to pour his feelings out to, but he was painfully shy, especially around women.

In an attempt to try and 'normalise' his life, in his mid-twenties José Luis finally began trying to date girls. Some of the women later said he was a much better listener than most Mexican men and a lot more handsome. But José Luis lacked the confidence to take the initiative with any of those early relationships.

In 1996 – aged 27 – he met a woman called Aide in a Mexico City bar and, because she seemed so kind and considerate, he became almost instantly smitten. He later said it was the first time in his life that he found himself actually trusting a woman. He hoped that Aide would help him evolve into becoming a more well-rounded person, in spite of his troubled background.

José Luis even quit working as a clown and found himself a regular job in a factory. The couple rented a small apartment and he seemed to become a much happier and calmer character. After just a few months as a couple, they decided to get married.

A child soon followed. José Luis told one friend at the time he couldn't believe how lucky he'd been to meet someone like Aide. The pair were just as delighted when she got pregnant for a second time.

However, just a few weeks after the birth of their second daughter, José Luis arrived home from work to find Aide in tears. While she didn't say anything at the time, he presumed she'd been struggling to cope with two young children. But a few days later, Aide broke down again and admitted to José Luis she'd met someone else and she planned to move to the United States with him.

José Luis was devastated. His marriage had helped him get rid of that inbuilt hatred of women caused by his mother. Now, he was once again filled with contempt for all females and wondering why he'd trusted any of them in the first place.

After his wife Aide left, José Luis unsurprisingly fell into a deep depression. He was all alone in the world again and the resentment he'd felt as a child returned.

The job he'd taken in a factory was supposed to reassure Aide he'd always support her and their children, but now it meant nothing. He hated the monotony of his work and now there was no reason to be there either.

José Luis had harboured dreams of becoming an artist ever since he'd worked as a clown and would spend his spare time immersed in poetry and literature. Now, with no one to support and a bleak-looking future, he decided to reinvent himself as an artist. At least that way he could be a *somebody* as opposed to a *nobody*.

With his handsome, rugged features, José Luis found it relatively easy to convince people he met that he was a creative type. He grew his hair longer and bought colourful, unusual clothing in second-hand stores. But he couldn't escape the feelings of loneliness and abandonment that had come from his wife running away with their two children, so he once again began drinking heavily.

This time he also began taking drugs, which he found helped give him the confidence to convince people he was a poet and a writer. In addition to poetry, he started reading a lot of literature about black magic and the occult. He was curious about it and felt drawn to it because it seemed to have a connection to many of his most disturbing child-hood memories.

Gradually, José Luis began making a modest living selling his paintings and poetry on the streets of Mexico City. His good looks and soft, gentle, hesitant voice convinced a lot of people (especially younger people) that he was genuine.

He soon began picking up 'followers' among the free-thinking, idealistic students attending colleges in and around the centre of Mexico City. One of the women who fell under his spell was Lydia Sanchez Valdez.

From the moment they first met, Lydia found José Luis intriguing and mysterious. He seemed so different from all the other men she'd dated. She could tell from his obsessive, compulsive personality that he was troubled and in need of emotional help, and that vulnerability made him more appeal-ing to her in many ways.

Lydia ignored the manic way José Luis kept his tiny apartment spotlessly clean and how he proudly announced that he washed himself from head to toe at least twice a day. She actually found it endearing, as most Mexican men were the opposite when it came to personal hygiene.

José Luis and Lydia appeared an attractive, happy, well-suited couple to everyone they met during the early stages of their relationship. And so none of Lydia's friends were surprised when José Luis asked her to marry him.

Just a few days after they'd tied the knot, Lydia stumbled on some witchcraft and black magic books in a chest in their bedroom. At first, Lydia convinced herself it was an interest for her new husband rather than an obsession.

She had no idea that José Luis had been trying to avoid his own demons for many years and this had clearly drawn him into the world of the occult. But when Lydia tried to tackle José Luis about these interests, he was irritated because he considered it none of her business. He accusing her of spying on him and then realised she was acting like his mother in many ways, which had no doubt sparked his anger in the first place.

This realisation stopped him shouting at Lydia and instead he began suffering immense feelings of guilt about having been horrible to her. This reaction was so sudden and all-consuming that José Luis found himself seriously considering committing suicide. 'I realised this was all my fault and the ghosts of my childhood would never stop haunting me,' he later explained.

It became clear to Lydia that her husband's anger and frustration was hiding many demons from his past. When she tried to talk to José Luis about it, though, he got angry again. Later he said it was because he felt as if she were attacking him, like his mother had so often done during his childhood.

José Luis eventually told Lydia about his suicidal thoughts. He also warned her he'd kill himself if she ever left him, given what he'd been through with his first wife.

Lydia pulled back from splitting up with José Luis and instead tried to help him. She even managed to get him to open up more about his childhood. But José Luis was on an emotional cliff edge, unsure which way to jump. When Lydia arranged for him to see a therapist, he walked out of the first session minutes after it started.

Back home in their apartment, his temper worsened and he came close to hitting Lydia on a number of occasions. But she continued trying to help him and assured him she'd remain by his side as long as they kept trying to work things through.

But then José Luis shut down again and refused to talk about his feelings any more. When Lydia pressed him, he grabbed her by the neck and began choking her until she almost lost consciousness. He then stormed out of their apartment, leaving her dazed on the sofa.

The following day, José Luis arrived back at the apartment to find Lydia packing her bags, about to leave. He burst into tears and begged his wife not to go but she told him that his therapist had already warned her that he was close to breaking point and might hurt her. It was too dangerous for her to stay.

José Luis was so shocked by what Lydia told him that he agreed to immediately leave the apartment while she finished packing her bags. That night he returned to the empty flat all alone yet again. He knew his childhood had caused a lot of what was happening but that didn't make it any easier for him to deal with. He later said that by this time he felt that he didn't deserve anyone's love, although he still longed for a genuine relationship and everything that went with it.

Back in his small apartment on his own, José Luis once again buried himself in poetry and read at least one book each and every week. He scraped together enough money to survive by selling his art and poetry on the streets. At least he was still able to convince others he was an idealistic novelist, actor, painter and poet.

To other, older people he encountered, José Luis started passing himself off as a television personality and sometimes even a TV news reporter. But in reality, he was nothing more than a street drifter begging for money in exchange for ham-fisted, clichéd poetry and a handful of clumsy, childish-looking paintings.

José Luis couldn't afford to visit any bars or nightclubs, so most of his encounters with other people occurred on the pavements and in the stores close to his small apartment. Many of those who encountered him at this time later said he seemed distant and depressed. But he still came across women who found his vulnerability attractive, especially when he insisted on writing specific, personal poems for them.

One woman José Luis met after splitting up from wife Lydia later recalled that she felt so sorry for him that she agreed to help him sell his paintings and handmade printouts of his novels and poems often for as little as a dollar in Mexico's busy city centre.

His latest girlfriend didn't realise that most of the cash she helped José Luis earn was being spent on cocaine and alcohol, which made him more jealous and controlling. He soon became paranoid that she would leave him.

One evening in the apartment, José Luis hysterically threatened to cut his own wrists in front of his girlfriend after she worked out that his mental health problems weren't just down to his abysmal childhood, but also down to being confused about his own sexuality. The pair split up and José Luis began sleeping with men as well as women. He insisted to one friend that he believed he was actually 100 per cent gay but slept with women to try and convince himself he was straight.

One of José Luis's new male lovers in Mexico City introduced him to a 32-year-old single mother of two called Alejandra Galeana, who happened to work at José Luis's local pharmacy. When they met, he introduced himself by saying: 'My name is José Luis Calva Zepeda.'

She later recalled: 'He made it sound as if I should have heard of him.'

And when Alejandra asked him what he did for a living, he looked affronted and answered her indignantly: 'Poet, playwright and singer.'

Moments later, he showed her his paintings and poetry. Alejandra became hooked on him and he seemed to her to be such a 'gentle, free spirit'. When José Luis announced to Alejandra that he was dropping his paternal surname and wanted to be simply known as 'José Zepeda', it endeared him to her even more.

José Luis's small apartment perfectly matched his image as a struggling writer and artist in Mexico City. It was located just a few blocks from the famed Plaza Garibaldi, in the centre of the city where mariachi musicians and other street artists often gathered.

He sold his art, poetry and books at some of the city's informal flea markets. He told Alejandra he was also a screenwriter and had written a script for a horror film, although he never actually showed it to her.

By this time, José Luis was addicted to clonazepam, cocaine and alcohol. Often, he'd take all three at the same time before heading out on to the streets to pick up new 'disciples'. Clonazepam was a potent, highly addictive, anti-seizure medication used to treat anxiety.

He began stealing clonazepam tablets from the pharmacy where Alejandra worked whenever she wasn't looking. But she didn't know about this, and so Alejandra felt secure enough about their relationship to invite him to lunch at her mother's home on the outskirts of Mexico City in September 2007.

Housewife Soledad Garabito Fernández wasn't as impressed by this vain man in his late thirties as her daughter Alejandra, though. Soledad later recalled that she disliked José Luis from the moment she first set eyes on him. She couldn't actually put a finger on why. He just irritated her intensely. But like so many parents, she didn't tell her daughter this because she didn't want to upset her.

Throughout the meal at her apartment, 55-year-old Soledad watched José Luis very closely and kept noticing how glazed his eyes were most of the time.

'He didn't really notice anyone or anything around him,' she later recalled. 'He just seemed only interested in himself.'

Soledad also never forgot how José Luis couldn't stop talking. He barely paused for breath as he outlined his supposedly glamorous, creative life to Soledad and her daughter.

She explained: 'He just kept saying over and over again he was a poet, as well as a playwright, a director and a singer. He even boasted that he earned $200 a day selling his written works. But I knew it couldn't be true because his clothes were so tattered.'

As José Luis had lunch that Sunday with Soledad and her daughter Alejandra, he took twice as long to eat his food as them because he was talking so much.

'He lived only in his world and no one else's,' Soledad added. 'He didn't ask either of us a single question. It was all about him.'

Soledad felt José Luis was constantly trying to prove something to both her and her daughter. He also never gave either of them enough time to question the accuracy of what he was saying by rapidly jumping from subject to subject.

Soledad later added: 'I concluded he was a bit of a creep. He had no charm whatsoever and I couldn't believe my daughter even liked him. Everything was "me, me, me".'

Over the following weeks, further disturbing clues about José Luis's real, severely damaged personality began to emerge. Whenever Alejandra was away from José Luis working in the local pharmacy, he harassed her with constant phone calls threatening to commit suicide if she ever tried to break off their relationship.

Then one evening Alejandra was on her way home from her job when she noticed José Luis secretly following her. When she confronted him in the street, he yelled at her and then grabbed her by the arm and accused her of cheating on him.

He seemed about to hit her when he broke down in tears and insisted he was only following her to make sure she was not in another relationship. Alejandra pushed José Luis away and ran off into a crowd of people walking nearby to escape his attention.

Alejandra went to her mother's apartment and told her what had happened. Soledad said she must immediately end the relationship.

Alejandra called José Luis on the phone that night and told him that it was over. The following day she persuaded her bosses at the pharmacy to immediately transfer her to another store on the other side of the city, well away from José Luis's apartment.

When he found out, he phoned Alejandra up in a fury and demanded to know why she was not working in the same pharmacy. She told him she was scared of him and repeated that their relationship was over.

But José Luis refused to accept it and kept insisting over and over again that he was in love with her. He begged her not to leave him, even though at the time he was also sleeping with men, as well as looking out for other women to seduce. In addition to losing another partner, he was distraught that he wouldn't have access to any more clonazepam tablets.

One of José Luis's former male lovers later recalled: 'He treated his supposed girlfriends as if they were the sexually submissive partners in each relationship. I remember how he told me that he'd say things to them like, 'Who told you you could talk?' He told me he liked the feeling that he owned those women.'

Around this time, José Luis wrote a disturbing short story entitled 'The Night Before'. In it, he said: 'I'm going to imagine myself as a balloon the size of the sun, and I'm going to roll around in the cosmos.'

The same former lover added: 'He really believed he was cleverer than all of us and that no one in the entire cosmos would ever work out what he was doing.'

Over the following months, José Luis charmed his way into the life of another woman called Veronica R, who was an assistant in the same pharmacy where Alejandra had worked before her transfer. José Luis read poetry to her in the store. She later admitted: 'He seemed to have an amazing personality and used it to charm me.'

But neither Alejandra nor Veronica realised that José Luis had also courted both of them in order to continue to get access to clonazepam. He recognised they were from relatively poor backgrounds, which he believed made them much more vulnerable and easier to dominate and control, and he needed this almost as much as he needed the drugs.

At the same time as all this, José Luis was also in the middle of a serious relationship with a man called Juan Carlos Monroy Pérez. He told friends that José Luis fervently denied being gay throughout their friendship and often turned violent if challenged about his sexuality.

On 5 October 2007, José Luis's one-time girlfriend Alejandra Galeana didn't show up for work at the pharmacy where she'd moved to get away from José Luis. She also didn't go to her mother Soledad's house later the same day where her two young children were being looked after.

Her mother immediately suspected that José Luis was behind her daughter's disappearance. She later recalled: 'I was certain he was involved somehow. But I figured that maybe he'd tied her up somewhere under the influence of some drug in order to stop her from going out.'

When Soledad reported her suspicions to the police and appealed for help, they weren't remotely interested. One officer even suggested that Alejandra had probably run off with her lover José Luis.

Soledad was so convinced the officers were wrong that she started her own investigation into her daughter's disappearance. She printed up posters featuring a photo of Alejandra and mentioning her daughter's nicknames 'Blondie' and 'Ale' for short.

Then Soledad headed for the apartment block where José Luis lived. Neighbours told her that on the day Alejandra went missing, they'd noticed José Luis and a young woman who matched Alejandra's description enter his apartment building.

Armed with this concrete evidence, Soledad marched back into her local police station and demanded action. This time officers responded and headed straight round to José Luis's dingy fourth-floor apartment. When no one answered the front door, six officers forced the front door open.

Inside, they found José Luis in the kitchen basting some unusual-smelling cutlets in a frying pan with fresh lemon juice. When they asked him why he hadn't answered the door, he just shrugged his shoulders and said he was starving hungry.

He nodded casually when they asked him if they could search the apartment.

As José Luis continued cooking, the officers headed to his bedroom where they immediately noticed a pungent aroma coming from a closet. Inside it, they discovered a dismembered corpse. Two grim-faced officers immediately returned to the kitchen to find José Luis serving strips of cooked meat from a frying pan on to a plate. He barely responded as they handcuffed him.

Inside the refrigerator, the officers discovered a right forearm and right leg which had been cut just below the knee. Next to the remains was a corn flakes box containing a bone covered in muscle tissue that seemed to have already been deep-fried in batter.

José Luis watched all this while standing in handcuffs between two uniformed policemen. One officer later recalled that José Luis kept shrugging his shoulders, as if to say he had no idea what was happening.

Another policeman later recalled: 'He just didn't seem bothered by what we'd found. In fact, in some ways he looked almost proud.

'He also didn't express any empathy or sorrow for what he'd done. It was as if everything in that apartment was all perfectly normal.'

One officer became so frustrated by José Luis's lack of response that he lost his temper, grabbed José Luis by the collar and was about to hit him when two colleagues pulled the angry officer out of the room. When the remaining police calmly asked José Luis what had happened, he stated in a casual, matter-of-fact tone that he'd accidentally choked Alejandra to death during a furious row two nights earlier.

It was only then that the police officers realised he must have been cooking her body parts in the frying pan when they arrived at the apartment.

On the floor of the entrance to José Luis's bedroom, two policemen noticed a pair of trainer shoelaces. They were bagged as evidence as the officers suspected that José Luis had used the laces to strangle his victim.

Inside a large box in the bedroom, police found an assortment of bloodstained knives, a box cutter and the trainers without shoelaces. José Luis insisted to the officers in his apartment that he hadn't actually eaten any parts of Alejandra's body and that he'd been intending to feed the remains to stray dogs in the neighbourhood. But one investigator noticed that his eyes kept glancing nervously around the room, which convinced them that he was lying.

When two officers left the kitchen to continue their search of the apartment, José Luis pushed the policeman left guarding him to the floor and lunged through open French windows out onto a small balcony. Despite still being in handcuffs, José Luis tried to scramble over the railings. As officers appeared on the balcony, he lost his footing and fell more than 10 feet on to a concrete floor of another balcony below.

Police officers peering over the edge saw José Luis sprawled out on the ground writhing in agony, convinced his leg was broken. Three police officers entered the apartment below and dragged José Luis off the balcony, still in handcuffs. They took him in a police van to a local hospital to get treatment for his injuries.

Back in José Luis's apartment, other officers continued their search. Among the items they uncovered was an unfinished novel he'd written entitled *Cannibal Instincts*. On its cover page was a masked image of fictional serial killer Hannibal Lecter, the flesh-eating psychopath from the hit series of bestselling novels that included *The Silence of the Lambs*.

José Luis had superimposed a photo of his own face on to the book cover. This act of seemingly ultimate narcissism proved Soledad's theory that José Luis only ever thought about himself.

As investigators closely examined the book, they began to wonder if he'd killed and eaten his victim as research for his books and film scripts. He'd even written down all his thoughts and responses to every evil act committed in the book.

This evidence eventually enabled police to link José Luis to two more murders. One was a former girlfriend called Verónica Consuelo Martínez Casarrubia, who disappeared in 2004. The other was a sex worker known locally as 'La Jarocha'. Both women's remains were found severely mutilated and dumped close to Zepeda's apartment. The bodies had had chunks of flesh hacked from them.

Investigators also uncovered José Luis's personal video collection, which included *The Silence of the Lambs* sequel *Hannibal* and a French film called *Cannibal Blood*.

Forensics who examined the cooked meat in José Luis's apartment confirmed they were the remains of his former girlfriend Alejandra. Evidence also clearly showed that José Luis had strangled her before cutting her corpse up into small strips. However, police did not carry out tests on José Luis's digestive system until 48 hours after his arrest, so they discovered no traces of her remains in his digestive system.

There was, though, ample evidence of José Luis's chronic addiction to clonazepam, cocaine and alcohol in his bloodstream. Following treatment at hospital for the injuries sustained when he fell from his balcony, José Luis was taken to a cell at the local police station. But he was so drowsy from the meds administered by doctors at the hospital that police decided to let him sleep off their effects before interrogating him.

As news spread throughout Mexico City about the arrest of this alleged serial killer and what police had found in his apartment, the local media rather unimaginatively dubbed José Luis the 'cannibal poet'.

When investigators finally confronted him about his crimes, he insisted that his main motivation in killing anyone was that he wanted 'to feel the pain' of his victims and the only way to do that was to experience the reality of what they went through.

The case rocked Mexico City's homicide police division because – despite a population of more than 20 million – there had not been a single cannibalism case in the city for more than 20 years.

Neighbours in the apartment block where José Luis lived told police and journalists that he was quiet and reserved, although the manager of a nearby pizza shop labelled him as: 'A hypocrite, someone very concerned with being accepted' after an argument about an unpaid bill.

In October 2007 – a few days after his original arrest – police investigators discovered the remains of a second prostitute who was known only as 'La Jarocha'. Her body parts were discovered in a dustbin near his apartment.

Police also disclosed details about how José Luis had decapitated his then-girlfriend Verónica Martínez Casarrubia before mutilating her body. They believed some of her remains were in two cardboard boxes, also dumped near his apartment. As in the case of José Luis's original victim Alejandra Galeana, the cause of death in each murder had been strangulation. José Luis insisted to police that he'd been in a romantic relationship with Verónica Martínez and denied any involvement in her murder or that of sex worker La Jarocha in April that same year.

While all these chilling details were being revealed in public for the first time, José Luis was transferred from his cell at the local police station to a secure mental hospital. Experts were ordered to put him through an extensive range of psychological tests to see what had driven him to kill in the first place, and to establish if he was mentally sane enough to be tried for his crimes.

Psychiatrists eventually concluded that José Luis was fit to stand trial but that he had been frustrated by his failure as a writer and artist. This had contributed to the rage he felt towards all women, as well as his childhood experiences at the hands of his mother.

As police began locating and interviewing José Luis's friends and family, they also discovered that he'd become increasingly interested in animal pornography and witchcraft, in addition to becoming obsessed by the classic sadist novel *120 Days of Sodom.*

A few days after José Luis's arrest, his one-time lover Juan Carlos Monroy Pérez was arrested by police. He admitted being in a relationship with the suspected serial killer in 2004, when he was believed to have killed some of his victims. Pérez was alleged by detectives to have been an accomplice to the murder of sex worker La Jarocha in April 2004.

Pérez admitted to police he knew José Luis had killed the divorced mother of three and then hacked her to pieces. But he insisted he'd played no part in the slaying. He claimed he'd been afraid to say anything in case he ended up being another victim.

At José Luis's first court appearances following his arrest, he refused to make a formal plea of guilty or not guilty and curtly informed the court: 'I can't get my thoughts together right now.'

He'd forgotten that he'd already confessed to police that he'd killed 32-year-old girlfriend Alejandra Galeana, as well as killing and dismembering at least two other women.

José Luis wasn't initially charged with any other killings, though, because police wanted to gather further evidence about other murders in order to present all the evidence to prosecutors in one package.

At a later court appearance, José Luis's newly appointed defence attorney Humberto Guerrero Plata insisted on his behalf: 'He killed her (Alejandra) because he was high on cocaine. He didn't eat her, he just cut her body up.'

But Mexico City coroner Rodolfo Rojo told the hearing that Alejandra's remains showed clear evidence that José Luis had meticulously separated and deboned his girlfriend's arm. He'd then carefully sliced off the skin so that he could fry the flesh and season it with lemon and chilli. Prosecutors insisted this 'preparation' of the body was far too elaborate to be for dog food, which had been what José Luis had claimed following his arrest.

Despite the graphic descriptions of his alleged crimes, there were journalists in court during José Luis's appearances who wrote more about his brooding good looks and dark, penetrating stare than his homicidal tendencies.

Prosecutors also presented to the court further psychological profiles of José Luis which described him as a chronic alcoholic and heavy cocaine user prone to bouts of depression, as well as someone who regularly attempted suicide. These experts concluded that José Luis was a man of average intelligence, who craved social acceptance but never actually achieved it.

One psychologist alleged that José Luis's hatred of solitude may have also driven him to kill his victims and eat some of their remains. Like other notorious cannibal serial killers Dennis Nilsen and Jeffrey Dahmer, José Luis wanted those remains to 'keep him company' because he was so lonely. It also meant his victims could never leave him.

The mental health expert told the court that the way José Luis's mother had destroyed that toy truck when he was a child had been one of the most damaging moments in his life. Other experts called by prosecutors claimed José Luis was being manipulative and had used that incident and others to try and camouflage the shame he felt after being raped by a friend of his mother's when he was seven years old.

Neither José Luis's mother Elia nor any of his siblings visited him in the hospital where he was admitted following his escape attempt or in the mental institution where he was in custody. They were also not present in court during his trial.

One detective later commented: 'His family didn't seem to care about him or his victims. They were incapable of showing any empathy. That explained a lot about how his own character developed. They simply didn't accept any responsibility for his crimes.'

José Luis's mother Elia later told reporters that she wanted nothing to do with her son ever again because of the shame he'd brought on the family name. One sister Claudia Fabiola refused to speak publicly about him.

When his elder brother, Jorge Calva Zepeda, was approached by journalists, his only comment was: 'My only crime is to have been the brother of José Luis.'

José Luis was eventually found guilty of Galeana's murder, as well as abusing a corpse. He was convicted on two further counts of murder and sentenced to 84 years in prison.

After being locked up in the Reclusorio Oriente prison to serve his sentence, José Luis refused to leave his cell and spent much of the time pacing up and down, which further worsened the insomnia he'd been already suffering from since his arrest.

One psychologist who examined Zepeda in prison following his sentencing concluded that the extreme hallucinations he was experiencing had been brought on by the realisation of what he'd done. But Mexican prison and justice officials refused to address José Luis's mental health issues and insisted he continue to serve his sentence in a prison.

José Luis eventually began working on a book about himself and his experiences in jail, tentatively entitled *The Cannibal Poet*. Those close to him said that writing the book helped improve his mental health, as he enjoyed pouring all his thoughts out on paper.

Other inmates in the same prison talked openly about how much they loathed José Luis. They accused him of making little effort to befriend them. Some said he was acting as if he was superior to them, as if he should be treated as an artist, rather than a mass murderer.

There were rumours circulating the prison that some inmates on José Luis's wing were convinced that their names would be revealed in the book he was writing and this was upsetting them. As word of the book spread through the prison, José Luis received direct death threats from a number of inmates. Other prisoners tried to blackmail him into paying them protection money every month to ensure he wasn't killed.

One inmate even claimed that José Luis deliberately refused to pay the protection money in the hope that it might cost him his life. The Mexican department of corrections later denied José Luis was ever threatened or beaten by other inmates.

On the morning of 11 December 2007, José Luis was found hanging by his belt from the ceiling of his cell inside the Reclusorio Oriente prison. He'd apparently committed suicide, although the circumstances behind his death were clouded in mystery. José Luis was supposed to have been under 24-hour surveillance, as he'd been considered a high-risk prisoner. Yet there were no guards around when he died.

José Luis's lawyer Moises Humberto Guerrero Calderon later said: 'He didn't seem to have suicidal tendencies any more and was very enthusiastic about (the book) idea. It seemed to be giving him a reason to live.'

Prison officials insisted José Luis could not have been murdered because he'd reinforced his locked cell door with wire and shoelaces tied from the inside. However, this was also a clear implication José Luis knew his life was under threat.

Mexico City prison officials later conceded that they were investigating how José Luis got the belt he used to kill himself with when he was supposed to be under round-the-clock observation. The forensic examination that was later done on José Luis's body did show that he'd been tortured and raped before he died. It was clear that his death wasn't a straightforward suicide as prison authorities had originally insisted.

Some inmates and staff later alleged that José Luis was killed because, given his mental health had deteriorated so badly, his fellow prisoners felt he was about to murder one of them, and so they all agreed he should be killed to prevent that happening.

As the investigation was going on, two inmates claimed to prison authorities that José Luis had persuaded a group of fellow inmates to kill him, because he wanted to make sure he definitely died. He was convinced prison guards would be obliged to rescue him if he tried to commit suicide as they'd done that on a number of occasions previously.

In interviews with journalists published after his death, José Luis openly expressed remorse for killing his ex-girlfriend Alejandra Galeana. He claimed that Alejandra was the love of his life and he never intended to kill her but found himself driven to do so by his confused psychological state at the time.

Alejandra's mother Soledad Garavito understandably dismissed such claims and told journalists: 'I don't wish death on anybody, but I feel this was divine justice. I do not take pleasure in this man's death, but I have seen there is a God and that He is with me.'

Many months after José Luis's death in prison, one of his sisters finally spoke out about her brother's death. She said that she and one of José Luis's former girlfriends were convinced the 'cannibal poet' was murdered by fellow prisoners encouraged by prison authorities.

This was once again denied by the prison. However, shortly after his death, a new director took over the Reclusorio Oriente and a fresh team of investigators re-examined José Luis's death. They eventually concluded that several of José Luis's fellow inmates most likely clubbed together and killed him, though no one was ever brought to justice for his alleged murder.

Mexican law enforcement authorities also conveniently announced around this time that they had concrete evidence linking José Luis to the murder of at least 10 more victims. Further investigations into these deaths allegedly committed by José Luis were eventually shelved after the authorities were accused of blaming him for a number of unsolved killings in order to 'clear the books' and improve Mexico City police homicide statistics.

Like so many other serial killers, José Luis had a split personality. There was the sad, lonely loser deluding himself and others that he was a sensitive artist and there was a brutal serial killer so deranged that he ate his victims to stop them leaving him.

But when these two extreme personalities clashed, there was an almighty explosion of violence which resulted in the deaths of many innocent people.

CHAPTER EIGHT

THE SADIST DOCTOR
RAÚL OSIEL MARROQUÍN REYES

From the moment he was born on 1 September 1980, Roberto Marroquín and Gloria Reyes gave their beloved son Raúl Osiel Marroquín Reyes every moment of their attention. They believed this would ensure he made a success of his life.

They encouraged an air of expectancy around young Raúl as he grew up in the town of Tampico, Mexico. But, perhaps as a result of this, Raúl seemed to look down his nose at most of his contemporaries at school, who found him arrogant and cold.

Raúl's over-attentive parents insisted he should ignore his classmates and work hard at school. They encouraged him even more when he told them he wanted to one day become a doctor.

But his decision was really down to their demanding expectations, which were so wide-ranging that Raúl felt obliged to impress his pushy parents just to keep them happy. He was so worried about letting them down that he became increasingly withdrawn and began preferring his own company to that of other people.

By the time Raúl had reached 13 years of age, he'd evolved into being a quiet, shy academic teenager who made his parents beam with pride. But underneath that normal exterior was an intense adolescent in turmoil about his own sexuality and the meaning of life.

Girls he met at this time found Raúl extremely awkward because he could barely make conversation with them. He later said that he'd spent so much of his early life inside his own head that he didn't know what was expected of him out in the real world.

Raúl's parents and other family members had no idea the teenager was going through such inner turmoil. They simply took him to be a bookish, serious young man with a fine academic career ahead of him. His shyness was given little thought or consideration.

And Raúl continued to be put under immense pressure from his mother and father to become a doctor through his adolescence. He didn't dare tell them that he was dreading the seven-year training that a career in medicine would require.

Raúl also knew that his parents couldn't really afford to send him through college, so he eventually convinced them to allow him to join the armed forces and then use the services to sponsor his training to become a doctor. This meant his parents would not have to pay hefty student fees, but he could still make them proud.

On 21 January 1999, Raúl enrolled as a private in the 15th Infantry Battalion of the Mexican Army in his home town of Tampico. He made it clear to his superiors that he fully intended to combine being a good soldier with studying medicine.

But question marks soon arose about Raúl's abilities as both a soldier and a trainee doctor. He struggled to participate in any of the army's standard team activities and was clearly unable to grasp the basic service requirements of loyalty and reliability.

Raúl's senior officers became convinced he was using the Mexican army to qualify as a doctor and then he'd quit, and eventually they withdrew their support for his medical training, proclaiming that he wasn't academically bright enough to pass the required exams.

Raúl knew how disappointed his parents would be, so he didn't dare tell them. His contemporaries in the army at that time later recalled that Raúl's personality drastically altered after he was rejected as a trainee doctor.

He began showing an open lack of respect towards his senior officers, being short-tempered and resentful when given orders. Many of Raúl's fellow soldiers avoided him and he gradually slipped back into becoming the same sort of loner he'd been throughout most of his childhood. And throughout, his simmering sexual appetite had returned to the surface. He later said that at the time he just couldn't stop thinking about sex.

During one army exercise in the desert in May 2004, two soldiers in Raúl's unit accused him of getting into bed with them in a tent in the middle of the night. They both claimed he tried to molest them.

When confronted with the allegations, Raúl explained that the incidents were the result of a misunderstanding and his superior officers believed him. But within 24 hours, a third similar incident was reported to them. Raúl was issued with a final warning that he'd be discharged if any more accusations were made against him.

Raúl became even more of a figure of hate inside his unit after news of the incidents spread through his army base. No one would talk to him and most soldiers muttered 'sicko' and 'pervert' under their breath whenever they walked past him.

When one confrontation between Raúl and two other soldiers resulted in guns being drawn and almost fired, Raúl's superior officers decided – just 10 days after that final warning – that he should be discharged from the army immediately.

Raúl had nowhere else to turn, so he travelled from the army base back to his home town of Tampico, although he was too ashamed to go back home to his parents and admit what had happened.

He drifted around the outskirts of the city carefully avoiding all the areas where he might bump into anyone he knew. He slept in ditches at night and scavenged discarded food from inside dustbins during the daytime. Raúl rapidly hit rock bottom as a broken, burned-out ex-serviceman.

When one childhood acquaintance recognised Raúl in the street, he denied who he was and angrily pushed the man away. Raúl then moved further out of the city to make sure no one else spotted him.

His only possession was a scruffy rucksack containing a few clothes and an army revolver he'd taken just before his discharge. He kept it for self-protection and had even waved it at a few people he thought were threatening him. But he never pulled the trigger.

Desperate and hungry, Raúl one day decided to use the gun to rob a local grocery store. But the owner produced a shotgun moments after Raúl pointed his weapon at him and Raúl was arrested by police and thrown in jail. He refused to tell officers where he'd got the gun but they soon established he'd stolen it from the army before his discharge.

The following day, Raúl was hauled in front of a judge and pleaded guilty to armed robbery. He was given a 14-month prison sentence.

The conditions inside prison were appalling and Raúl discovered it was impossible to get a proper meal without paying for it. His family never once came to see him and they refused to take reverse charge phone calls from him, so he had no way of getting any cash.

In the prison yard, a gang of older inmates surrounded him and told him they'd help him earn some money. All he had to do was sell his body to other inmates through them.

Raúl later said he was so shocked at first that he stormed away from the inmates. But minutes later they caught up with him in an unsupervised corner of the yard. He was told that unless he became a 'bitch' then he'd be killed. He had no choice. Raúl quickly discovered that no one within the prison administrative system cared that men were having to sell their bodies to other inmates in order to earn enough money to eat.

Isolated and lonely, Raúl became deadened to the reality of his dire predicament and tried to convince himself that sleeping with men was nothing more than a business transaction. In the army, Raúl had been labelled a 'pervert' because of those same sexual preferences. In prison, he did at least occasionally enjoy sleeping with men but only if they were kind to him. But he was constantly haunted by how, when he was a child, his father would drill it into him that if he ever 'turned faggot', his parents would kick him out of the home and disown him.

Raúl felt obliged to keep his relationships with men secret inside prison, which particularly suited the ones who had wives and families in the outside world. Some of the inmates were in such an extreme state of denial about their own sexuality that they'd take their frustrations out on Raúl and he ended up on the receiving end of some painful beatings. It was a time of great confusion for Raúl as he'd thought at least he'd be able to establish what his true sexual identity was, only to find himself being punished for taking such a path.

So by the time Raúl was released from prison he actually had an underlying hatred for gay men. He'd also presumed it would be safer to think that way in the outside world but he was in a more confused psychological state than when he'd entered prison.

Raúl was also desperate to avoid his home town of Tampico in case anyone – especially his family – found out that he'd slept with men in prison. He knew he needed to start again somewhere fresh.

Raúl had heard from other prisoners that Mexico City was a much more liberal society, so he moved there in the hope that he might meet someone and have a proper, loving relationship. Raúl arrived in the Mexican capital on 21 October 2005, and found himself drawn to the gay district of Zona Rosa, which had dozens of bars and clubs open 24 hours a day.

He ended up sitting at a bar sipping gently on a bottle of beer. It was so poorly lit that he could only just make out another customer in his late twenties sitting on a stool in the shadows glancing towards him. Juan Carlos Alfaro Alba tipped his bottle of beer in Raúl's direction and stared into his eyes for a few moments. Raúl nodded back.

The man sidled up next to Raúl at the bar and let his hand gently brush Raúl's thigh. They smiled at each other. Raúl later recalled that at that moment he felt completely confused. In one sense he was relieved someone even found him attractive but on the other hand he felt repulsed.

And when the conversation between them quickly turned to the other man's wealth, his family and career, Raúl later said that it felt to him like the man was demeaning him. This reminded him of several uncomfortable encounters back inside prison.

Raúl was also irritated that the other man clearly presumed that he wanted sex, as he didn't want to be thought of as an easy lay. Raúl later said that he decided at that moment to play the other man along to 'teach him a lesson'.

He suggested the other man pay for a hotel room for them. Juan Carlos thought he knew exactly what lay in store for him when – a few minutes later – he tried to grab Raúl's hand affectionately as they ascended in the hotel lift.

Within seconds of entering the room, Raúl overpowered Juan Carlos and tied him to a chair. Then he began interrogating him about being gay. When Juan Carlos started crying, Raúl smashed his fist into the other man's gut over and over again until he was screaming in pain.

More beatings and verbal abuse continued through the night until dawn, when Raúl forced Juan Carlos to give him the phone number of his parents. Raúl called them and coolly demanded that they pay him a ransom if they ever wanted to see their son again.

Juan Carlos's mother and father didn't dare contact the police in case it cost their son his life. An envelope containing thousands of dollars was delivered to the hotel reception later that morning.

Despite having got the cash, and very easily as well, Raúl decided to punish Juan Carlos and his parents further so he refused to let him go and even forced his prisoner to pay in advance for four more days in the room.

During that time, Raúl systematically beat and abused his prisoner. When he was finished, Raúl carefully wiped down all surfaces and other evidence in the hotel room and then left tied-up Juan Carlos slumped to one side on his chair. His face was bloody and swollen and he was barely conscious.

Raúl later recalled how he walked down the hotel corridor towards the lift that night almost skipping with delight. Not only had he made thousands of dollars but he also believed that he'd just proved to himself he wasn't gay after all.

* * *

Raúl spent some of the money he earned from the kidnapping on renting a small one-bedroom apartment at 4223 Avenida

Andrés Molina Enríquez, in the Venustiano Carranza district of Mexico City. Within days, he began to feel the urge to do it all over again, but he told himself that this time he was going to do things differently.

That evening, Raúl picked up another man and lured him back to his new apartment with a promise of sex. Within minutes of arriving there, Raúl had tied the man to the bed and was beating him.

Raúl eventually stopped and looked down at the other man sprawled out on his bed in just his underpants. His victim pleaded with him not to hurt him any more and offered him money.

But this time Raúl didn't even bother with that. He grabbed the man by the throat and began squeezing tightly. Then he used his full weight to push the palm of his hand down into the man's windpipe, crushing it until his victim lay limp and lifeless on the bed.

Raúl later recalled that the act of killing had given him an immense feeling of sexual relief. His hands were no longer shaking and even the headache he'd suffered since earlier that evening had gone. Raúl said that he believed he had the right to kill because that man had presumed he would have sex with him.

By the time Raúl 'came down' from the high of that first kill a few days later, he'd concluded that earning money by chatting up men in a gay bar and promising them sex was an easy way to make a fortune.

For his next target, Raúl visited a well-known Zona Rosa gay bar called the Cabaretito Neón. There, he tried and failed to pick up one man before successfully hitting on another, older customer sitting nearby. Raúl invited the man for a drink at his apartment and within moments of getting there Raúl overpowered him and tied him up.

The following morning his victim's wife was rung up by Raúl demanding a ransom. Within 24 hours, the cash had been delivered to the apartment but Raúl didn't bother calling the wife back to arrange for her husband to be picked up.

Instead, he strangled his victim with his bare hands and then laid the body out on a plastic sheet on the floor of the apartment. Using a huge kitchen knife, he cut the corpse into small enough pieces to be fitted into a black suitcase, which Raúl then dropped into a dustbin round the corner from the apartment.

A few days later, Raúl picked up another man in a small, seedy nightclub and lured him back to his apartment. He was tied up and gagged and a call was made to his family demanding money.

Once again, the ransom was quickly paid before Raúl murdered his victim. As the body lay on the floor of Raúl's apartment, he took out a razor blade and carefully sliced the skin off the forehead making sure to draw the clear outline of a bloody star. He wanted the police to think a religious cult had been responsible for the killing when they found his victim's remains. Less than an hour later, Raúl dumped the remains of the corpse in a garbage container located down a darkened alleyway near his apartment block.

The majority of Raúl's victims had kept their sexuality secret from their families, which meant some relatives were reluctant to report the kidnappings to the police. And even when they did, a lot of police officers were so homophobic that they didn't bother making much effort to find any trace of the missing men anyway.

Raúl's modus operandi was nearly always the same. He'd approach men in bars and establish through conversation if they or their relatives had enough money to pay a ransom before luring them back to his apartment.

He asked between 15,000 pesos ($1,500) and 120,000 pesos ($12,000) for each kidnapping victim, depending on their apparent wealth. He even filmed some killings with a video camera, which he liked to later play back to himself while he lay masturbating in bed.

Even when some human remains began turning up in dustbins, the police showed little interest. They had no idea the victims had been killed by the same person.

In October 2005, Raúl deliberately moved his hunting grounds away from the gay bars of the Zona Rosa because he feared the police might connect the area to the missing men.

In a grocery store, Raúl picked up a 32-year-old television producer and lured him back to his flat. Then, after receiving a ransom payment, murdered his victim.

Next came a 20-year-old student who met Raúl outside a fast-food joint. His body was found dumped next to a railway line close to a metro station.

A few days later, Raúl picked up a 28-year-old waiter working in a restaurant. The two men ended up in a room at a nearby hotel, where Raúl bound the man's hands and feet before demanding and receiving a ransom payment from his family. He then strangled his victim and dumped his body in a reservoir.

By this time, the police had been contacted by many more relatives of missing men and had to reluctantly concede there might be a serial killer in Mexico City who was murdering men after forcing their relatives to pay ransoms.

Alerts were posted on the streets and inside clubs across the Zona Rosa warning men to be very careful if approached by a stranger. The media portrayed the killer as being a homophobic psychopath who cruelly extracted money from his victim's relatives, believing that many would not go to the police because of the shame attached to their sexuality.

But none of this negative publicity disturbed Raúl, who later admitted he felt no guilt about what he was doing. One criminologist suggested that Raúl felt 'obliged' to keep hurting all gay men because of the way he'd suffered in prison, despite his own true sexuality.

Raúl would later say he liked throttling his victims until they passed out and then slapping them back into consciousness. Then he'd watch the relief in their eyes, which would then turn to terror as he began squeezing their necks again until they died.

On the evening of 27 October 2005, Raúl had just failed to chat up two men in a bar when a handsome younger man called 'Pedro' sidled up next to him in a very flirtatious manner. Pedro was a street hustler who'd survived for years drifting around Mexico City picking up men and then robbing them. He had watched Raúl failing to pick up the two men and decided he knew how to improve Raúl's chat-up techniques.

Minutes after Raúl and his new hustler friend began talking, they attracted the attention of an older man called Jonathan Razo Ayala, who was sipping on a Martini at the other end of the bar. Both men moved either side of their target and started flirting with him.

After luring Ayala to Raúl's apartment, the two men tied him up and demanded a $5,000 ransom from his family. But Ayala's parents told the kidnappers they couldn't afford to pay anything.

Over the following two weeks, Raúl and Pedro continually called the increasingly distraught family to try and get them to pay the ransom, but they insisted over and over again they had no money.

On 12 November 2005, the pair decided to murder their victim anyway, fearful that the family might call in the police. His remains were dumped a few streets away from the apartment.

Two weeks later – on 30 November 2005 – Raúl and Pedro were so desperate for cash they lured a man called Ricardo López Hernández back to Raúl's apartment with the promise of sex.

He was held captive in the apartment for nine days while his family raised a $2,000 ransom. Then on 9 December – hours after the money had been delivered to the apartment – Raúl told Pedro that they were going to kill Hernández.

His accomplice tried to stop him after pointing out that if Raúl murdered all their victims then the families would soon stop paying ransoms, as they'd know their loved ones would end up dead anyway. When Raúl ignored the advice and began strangling Hernández, Pedro tried to stop him and the two men ended up grappling on the floor in front of their terrified victim.

Raúl eventually punched Pedro so hard that he fell back on to the corner of a coffee table and was knocked unconscious. When he came around a few minutes later, Hernández was already lying dead on the sofa and Raúl was about to start cutting up the body.

Pedro sprang to his feet and ran out of the apartment, slamming the front door on his way out. He later said he was terrified that Raúl would come after him and kill him.

Meanwhile, Mexico City police's attempts at tracking down the serial killer had quickly fizzled out. Most detectives based in the Zona Rosa area of Mexico City were even refusing to visit gay clubs and bars as part of their investigation. Occasionally, family members of the victims would appeal through the media to the police to step up their enquiries, but detectives still seemed indifferent to the murders being committed almost under their noses.

In the middle of December 2005 – a few days after Hernández's murder – Raúl called his hustler friend Pedro and pleaded with him to come back to the apartment. He promised not to kill any more people. Pedro returned to the apartment and the following evening Raúl went out to find another victim because both men were broke.

At a bar in the Zona Rosa, Raúl picked up two more men. After establishing they were wealthy, all three went to Raúl's apartment, where Pedro lay in wait.

Both men were immediately gagged and tied up, and their families were contacted to pay ransoms. Once the money had been delivered to the apartment, Raúl stunned Pedro by murdering both men, in spite of his pledge not to kill anyone.

Pedro later told police that Raúl had confided in him that he actually kept a secret collection of trophies from each of his victims hidden in the apartment. These included voter credentials as well as pieces of jewellery and watches.

Raúl tried to placate Pedro on the night of those two murders by agreeing that killing all their kidnap victims did not make sense and he promised on his mother's life he would not do it again. So as a twisted gesture of good faith towards his friend, Raúl resisted the temptation to kill the next two victims after their families paid a combined ransom of $11,500.

The two survivors later claimed they were so scared that Raúl and his accomplice would come after them if they went to the police that they never reported what had happened.

On 13 December 2005, Raúl persuaded a man called José Ricardo Galindo Valdés to go back to his apartment where his friend lay in wait. When he rang his latest victim's terrified mother, she begged him not to hurt her son and insisted the family had no money to pay a ransom.

Raúl's accomplice Pedro pleaded with him to let this victim live. Raúl threatened to kill the man if he ever spoke to anyone about what had happened and he was allowed to leave the apartment unharmed.

Just three days later – on 16 December 2005 – another man was lured back to Raúl's apartment. This time the victim was murdered as soon as a ransom was paid. Pedro was so upset he stormed out of the apartment and said this time he was never coming back. But a month later Raúl managed to persuade Pedro to come back and live with him again after promising him a bigger share of the ransom money from each victim.

On 23 January 2006, the pair lured another man back to Raúl's flat. This victim's family were very wealthy and agreed to pay $20,000, one of the largest ever ransom demands by the pair.

Raúl went with Pedro to collect the ransom money from a nearby phone box. Raúl was so excited by the prospect of getting such a large amount of money that he didn't even bother to properly check the vicinity for police.

Moments after Raúl entered the phone box, a unit of armed police from Mexico City's Federal Investigation Agency (AFI), the *Federales*, swooped. They'd been alerted by the family of the latest victim.

Watching all this from a street corner and realising the police had spotted him, Pedro fled down a nearby narrow cobbled street. He was never tracked down despite a massive police sweep of the neighbourhood. When Raúl was searched, he was found to be in possession of many of his victims' voter credentials, which by this time he carried with him everywhere to remind him of his crimes.

The following day, the police announced that Raúl – just 25 years of age – was 'most likely responsible' for dozens of kidnaps and murders of men, although initially police only charged him in relation to the kidnap and murder of the two 23-year-old men taken hostage the previous month. Their cut-up bodies had been found crammed into a suitcase discovered on Avenida Andrés Molina Enríquez, in the Asturias district of Mexico City.

Police eventually charged Raúl with six kidnappings and four homicides. He insisted to detectives that he wasn't homophobic and had only targeted homosexuals because they were easy to 'hook up' with. He refused to talk about his accomplice Pedro, who'd disappeared.

But within days, Raúl told a journalist who visited him in prison that the murders he'd committed would be 'good for society'. This ensured he was branded as the ultimate homophobe in the media, who nicknamed him 'Sadic' and 'El Sadico' – both meaning 'the sadist'.

When Raúl was asked by the same journalist if he felt sympathy for the relatives of the people he'd murdered, he simply replied: 'I have never thought about them.'

One officer who attended the first interrogation of Raúl later recalled that he 'never showed one inch of regret. It was all a game to him.'

Raúl told the detective: 'One of my victims was a carrier of HIV, and in a certain way, I helped prevent the spread of the virus …'

Raúl described each murder as an 'operation' as if it were a military manoeuvre, and he admitted to detectives that he enjoyed torturing and inflicting pain on his victims as he saw it as a challenge to break the will of each one. This, he claimed, gave him absolute power over that person.

There is little doubt among the experts who have studied Raúl's chilling crimes that they were closely linked to his own sexual repression; a twisted form of payback because of the way he'd been assaulted by men inside prison.

Criminologists and other psychoanalysts who met him said Raúl lacked all empathy and believed himself to be far superior to most people. He'd never considered that he might get caught and also never accepted full responsibility for his brutal crimes. For a long time after his arrest, Raúl continued to claim that he had 'got rid of' his victims 'for the good of society'.

Raúl's reign of terror lasted for the duration of the year 2005. This is unusual in itself, as most serial killers spend years on the loose murdering multiple victims with impunity.

Raúl's much anticipated trial finally began in early September 2008. He was convicted of four charges of murder, kidnapping and hate crimes and sentenced to 300 years in prison.

After his sentencing, Raúl informed reporters at the court that if he was given the chance, he would kill again. But he said that next time, he would 'refine his methods' so he could manage to evade arrest.

'I would do it again,' he told journalists. 'But I'd be more careful not to get caught and not make the same mistakes. The only thing I regret is what my family is going through now.'

Reports that Raúl's accomplice Pedro was eventually arrested in a police raid in 2013 were later denied by prosecutors. But they did eventually acknowledge that Pedro had tried to stop Raúl at one stage, so he was not as culpable as his friend.

Raúl was initially sent to the Reclusorio Oriente jail in Mexico City. But in 2010 he was transferred to the more secure Santa Martha Acatitla Penitentiary, in Mexico City, following rumours that he was planning an escape. He is not expected to ever be released from prison. The whereabouts of his alleged accomplice Pedro are not known.

CHAPTER NINE

'EL HAMBURGUESA'
DAVID AVENDAÑO BALLINA

The slums of Mexico City were so derelict during the 1970s that the government of the time was accused of deliberately ignoring the poor in the hope that the death rate would rise and that a lot of the city's most broken citizens would simply perish. Plagues of rats were said to be better fed than the majority of slum dwellers, which was why the only way to survive in the ghetto was to beg, borrow and steal.

Six-year-old David Avendaño Ballina knew all about such struggles. His father was long gone and his mother had to sell her body on the streets to keep the family afloat.

David committed his first burglary just before his seventh birthday. He and an older boy broke into a run-down apartment belonging to an older female neighbour. The pair only realised she was in when they smelt food cooking.

They were about to enter the kitchen to investigate when the old lady appeared in a doorway and told them she was calling the police. The two boys looked at each other in desperation and went into a blind panic.

David's older accomplice grabbed a glass ashtray from a coffee table and smashed it repeatedly over the old lady's head until she collapsed unconscious on the floor in a pool of her own blood. The two boys then ripped the jewellery off her wrists, neck and fingers before scrambling towards the exit.

David later recalled that as they were about to open the front door of the apartment, he again smelt the food the old lady had been cooking and paused. He then walked back to the kitchen where he helped himself to the delicious meat stew simmering on the stove. It was the first proper hot meal he'd had in days.

As the older boy yelled at David to hurry up, he crammed so many spoonfuls of stew into his mouth that the gravy dribbled down his chin. Little David was about to take another mouthful when his partner in crime ran into the kitchen and dragged him out of the apartment, promising the starving younger boy he'd take him to the nearest hamburger joint.

Following that break-in and the fast-food meal which followed it, David was nicknamed 'El Hamburguesa' by his friends as news of the daring break-in spread through the barrio. In later life, El Hamburguesa hated the nickname because he felt it cast aspersions on his skills as a professional criminal, as well as highlighting the enormous waistline he ended up with when he was older.

El Hamburguesa rarely mentioned that the old lady died of those injuries inflicted by his accomplice during the break-in. But then El Hamburguesa rarely gave much thought to the consequences of any of his crimes. He later insisted that the only lesson he learned from that robbery was that it was always best to let others do your dirty work for you.

The boy who'd killed the old lady was eventually caught and sentenced to life in prison. He never informed on El Hamburguesa. The police knew who his accomplice was but didn't bother going after David because they knew he was so young that the Mexican justice system wouldn't properly deal with him, even if the evidence was there.

As a result, none of what happened during that murderous break-in put El Hamburguesa off pursuing a life of crime. He'd worked out by the age of 10 or 11 that he'd sooner climb the underworld ladder than bother with school, which seemed pointless to him. El Hamburguesa believed that his most important 'education' would be out on the mean streets of Mexico City rather than in the classroom.

By the age of 12, El Hamburguesa was out mugging pedestrians almost every night in his barrio and the richer central districts of the city. His nickname added to his fearsome reputation as an up-and-coming young criminal, because most folk in the barrio knew all about El Hamburguesa.

By the time he'd reached 15, El Hamburguesa had grown bigger and taller than most of the street criminals he was supposed to be looking up to. When El Hamburguesa beat up a street drug dealer so badly that he had to be hospitalised, one of the barrio's most notorious crime families were so impressed they recruited him as a henchman.

The mobsters believed that El Hamburguesa's toughness made him an ideal addition to their gang and he soon became renowned for never asking his bosses awkward questions. If he was ordered to do something for them, he simply went out and did it. As a result, El Hamburguesa was used by the crime family to 'discipline' any enemies who dared to cross them.

El Hamburguesa was so mature that he even proved his own leadership qualities by often getting other older gang members to carry out beatings on his behalf. But there was another important reason why the older mobsters liked having El Hamburguesa on their team: he had no criminal record. The local police knew only that the gang had a lethal new enforcer but they had no idea who he actually was, and this allowed him to move about and commit crimes quite freely.

El Hamburguesa further impressed his crime bosses by making it clear to them that he was even prepared to kill their enemies if necessary. He later boasted that he never refused to commit a killing on behalf of the gang. He believed it would further enhance his reputation and enable him to earn even more money.

Within just over a year of joining that local gang, teenage El Hamburguesa had personally shot dead four criminals on the streets of Mexico City.

'Killing became like a fix of heroin for me,' El Hamburguesa later explained. 'I knew I wanted to do it as much as possible. I got bored easily and killing helped keep me alert and on my toes. It was much more enjoyable than taking drugs.'

He craved the respect of his underworld associates, so whenever his bosses called him El Hamburguesa to his face it made him wince with irritation, as he saw himself as a valued member of the local cartel, rather than just some thuggish, fat gun for hire. He later said that if it hadn't been for his child-hood sweetheart Claudia Castillos Maya, he might have been tempted to hit back at his bosses. She taught him to watch his own back.

The pair first met when Claudia was working in a noto-rious Mexico City brothel and El Hamburguesa was a flashy young hood. He'd been wary of her at first because he knew from his own mother that sex workers targeted rich criminals in the hope they'd give them a better life. Claudia later admit-ted she had 'worked' on El Hamburguesa for many months after she first slept with him for money at the brothel, but then they gradually began to fall in love.

Claudia and El Hamburguesa married as soon as they both turned 18 and she urged her husband to quit the old local mob he belonged to and set up his own criminal gang.

She warned him he'd end up a marked man if he stayed with those old-timers and predicted that he'd most likely be killed doing their dirty work for them.

Claudia was so determined to get her new husband to start his own criminal organisation that she presented him with a 'business plan' which involved drugging prostitutes' clients and then ripping off all their cash and valuable possessions. Claudia also pointed out that if they had several 'teams' out at any one time trapping men, then they'd make a fortune.

El Hamburguesa's pushy wife also assured her young husband it would be easy money because most men who paid for sex were married. They wouldn't want their wives to know they'd been with another woman, so they'd be extremely reluctant to report such crimes to the police. When her husband pointed out to Claudia that drugging the men might be risky in case they died, she replied: 'Who cares if they die? They deserve it.'

El Hamburguesa was so careful not to upset his mobster bosses that he launched his new gang secretly. He didn't want to cut his ties with his current employer until he was sure this new racket would turn out to be as lucrative as wife Claudia believed.

The pair then visited several brothels in Mexico City to recruit women into their new gang. They wanted street-smart operators and both knew the women had to be good enough actresses to persuade the men to trust them from the moment they first met. The women would then administer drugs secretly into the men's drinks, knocking them out. Then all their valuables could be stolen.

El Hamburguesa and Claudia eventually cherry-picked 12 sex workers from the brothels they visited, plus male body-guards. They promised each woman she'd get 50 per cent of the takings from every job, although if there was a pair of women involved then their fee would come out of the same 50 per cent.

El Hamburguesa and Claudia assured all the women that the drugs they administered would only knock the men out for a short amount of time. And they insisted most victims wouldn't report what had happened to the police.

The priority of each team was to steal as much cash and valuables such as jewellery and watches as possible while their victims were unconscious, and El Hamburguesa's teams of femmes fatales were soon frequenting the busiest bars, canteens, restaurants and nightclubs in the centre of Mexico City.

They lured men to nearby hotels with the promise of sex. The women even implied they were looking for serious rela-tionships in order to convince the men to trust them.

Once in hotel rooms, the women made sure the men drank high ethyl spirits such as vodka or tequila and then squeezed a couple of ophthalmological drops containing benzodiazepine or cyclopentolate into those drinks. Within minutes these compounds would combine with the ethyl alcohol to suppress the men's nervous systems resulting in them feeling dizzy and weak before losing consciousness.

The first few jobs went exactly according to plan and the women were able to steal large quantities of cash and valuables. The crimes were not covered in the local newspapers, which further convinced El Hamburguesa and Claudia that few men would report the thefts to the police.

But then two men on successive evenings failed to recover consciousness and died. Both victims had all their belongings stolen, including money, cheque books and credit cards. The cards were maxed out within hours by El Hamburguesa's gang members. The victims' cars were even stolen, using their owner's keys before being sold on to specialist criminals.

The deaths of the two men in hotel rooms appeared initially to be down to natural causes, so the police were not called in to investigate until after the autopsy had been completed. Even then pathologists initially announced that both men had died from what they called 'generalised visceral congestion'. This was a form of asphyxia caused by something obstructing the victim's respiratory tract, which would then lead to a cerebral haemorrhage.

It was only when details of how the men's credit cards had been used by the gang started to emerge that police realised there was a possibility that a gang was responsible for both deaths, although they had no idea as to the identity of any of the actual criminals involved.

But out in Mexico City's underworld the gang had already been nicknamed 'Las Goteras', which in English means 'The Leaks'. This referred to the way El Hamburguesa's teams of criminals 'leaked' ophthalmological drops into their victims' drinks.

On 11 January 2005, a Mexican businessman called Julio César Albores Trujillo and his friend Francisco Ruiz Guízar invited four women they met in a Mexico City bar to his home in Colonia Cedros, in Coyoacán, on the edge of the city. Both men collapsed within minutes of arriving at the house and were robbed of all their most valuable belongings.

They eventually recovered consciousness, with no long-term side effects. But unlike previous victims, they went straight to the police to report what had happened. For whatever reason, officers completely failed to properly follow up their allegations.

Less than a month later – on 3 February 2005 – a man called Mariano Espinosa Falcón visited a dance hall in Plaza Garibaldi in the centre of Mexico City with his friend Erick Iván Martínez, and they picked up two women who then sat with them at their table in the club until dawn.

The two women agreed to go with the men to a hotel in nearby Colonia Guerrero. The women dropped poison into the men's drinks minutes after arriving in the hotel room. Erick Iván Martínez lost consciousness but his friend Mariano collapsed and died.

Police were alerted to the incident by the hotel manager who found both men after noticing the women leaving the premises in a hurry. But police investigators were begged by relatives of the man who'd died not to reveal his name to the press and so the story only got brief coverage in the media. A forensic examination of the body showed that the victim had died in a similar fashion to the previous cases.

Back at the home of El Hamburguesa and his wife Claudia, a couple of the women in the gang quit after being alarmed by the deaths of the victims. But the husband and wife ringleaders remained undeterred and had no doubt they could easily recruit more women. They also planned to increase the number of people in the gang so they could cover a wider area of the city and earn even more money.

El Hamburguesa and Claudia also launched operations in the states of Hidalgo, Tlaxcala, Guanajuato, Veracruz, Morelos, Puebla, Querétaro and Jalisco. But the police in Mexico City were still not prepared to officially confirm to journalists that the killings were the work of one gang.

In Mexico City, gang members met with El Hamburguesa and Claudio regularly in hotel rooms in the municipalities of Ecatepec and Nezahualcóyotl to discuss future jobs. They'd go through the details of all recent attacks and calculate how much money they'd earned. Flushed with the financial success of their crime spree, El Hamburguesa and Claudia also ordered their newly set up teams across the country to work a minimum of five nights a week.

In April 2007, gang members Susana Flores and Damaris Hernández chatted up two men in a Mexico City bar and agreed to go to one of the men's apartments in the Fraccionamiento Los Cedros de Coyoacán district, where they continued to party. After slipping drops into the men's drinks, the women collected all their cash and valuables and left the apartment block via a service lift to the street below, where they passed what they'd stolen to waiting male gang members. Back in the apartment, one victim was unconscious and the other man lay dead on the living-room floor.

The deceased man was the brother-in-law of the former governor of the state of Chiapas, and so suddenly the case became much more high profile. Under pressure from him, Mexico police finally launched a fully-fledged murder investigation into all the deaths.

Fingerprints from some of the most recent crime scenes were finally processed and found to match several members of the gang who had criminal records. The police confirmed in public for the first time that all the killings were most likely the work of one gang. However, while they knew they were likely looking for one group, investigators were not aware at this stage that El Hamburguesa and his wife Claudia were the masterminds behind the entire crime spree.

The suspects that were identified by fingerprints were hauled in for questioning and all initially denied any involvement in the poisonings. Further forensic evidence – including DNA taken from the crime scenes – proved they were lying and so, in May 2007, Mexico City police officially charged 11 men and 7 women with poisoning men after procuring them for sex. The same suspects then began offering information in exchange for reduced sentences. They referred to a man known only as El Hamburguesa as being their overall leader. Detectives also uncovered clear evidence that there were other cells of the gang operating in cities across the country.

Police eventually established El Hamburguesa's real identity and issued a warrant for his arrest in all the Mexican states where his gangs were operating. This included Jalisco, Querétaro, Hidalgo, Michoacán, Guanajuato and San Luis Potosí. El Hamburguesa – by this time aged 34 – avoided arrest by keeping on the move around Mexico, and so remained undetected.

Six months later – in February 2008 – he decided it was safe enough for him to start selling some of the leftover valuables his gang had earlier stolen on his behalf from their victims. When he tried to sell the items, though, the owner of the pawn shop he visited in the back streets of Mexico City's Historic Center recognised him from Wanted posters and called the police. Within minutes, El Hamburguesa was arrested by agents of the Capital Judicial Police on the corner of República de Uruguay and Eje Central.

El Hamburguesa was initially charged with organised crime offences, qualified homicide and aggravated robbery while police collected enough evidence to prove his involvement in the many murders connected to the crimes his gang had committed.

The police revealed to the media how El Hamburguesa's gang of women had 'hooked' their targets in restaurants, bars and nightclubs, stating also that the victims had mostly been aged between 20 and 38 years of age.

Detectives who interviewed El Hamburguesa following his arrest later recalled that he seemed openly proud and extremely empowered by the number of men murdered on his express orders. Some of the female members of his gang even told police that El Hamburguesa would become visibly excited when he heard details about each kill from them. They claimed that he continually assured them that it didn't matter if some of the victims ended up dying because 'they deserved it'.

As one investigator later said: 'He seemed to enjoy listening to the women recounting to him every sordid detail of the attacks and how the victims died.'

But another chilling motive lay behind the El Hamburguesa killings. Psychiatrists who later examined the case concluded that the victims may well have represented the men who'd abused David's mother after paying her for sex. Killing these men was El Hamburguesa's own twisted form of payback.

The press branded the gang as psychopaths and used the case to expose Mexico's secretive sex and vice trade, which had thrived in the shadows across the country for many decades. Many of the gang's innocent victims were also publicly demonised for hiring women for sex. Some members of the Mexican public insisted the victims deserved to die for being 'sinners' in the eye of God.

With El Hamburguesa, his wife Claudia and other gang members awaiting trials in separate prisons, detectives announced to the media that the entire gang had been taken off the streets, and thus they had no need to be concerned.

* * *

On 14 February 2009, 45-year-old sex worker María de los Angeles Sanchez Rueda, known as La Gorda (the fat one), and another woman called Estela González Calva La Tia picked up legendary Mexican wrestling brothers La Parkita and Espectrito Junior in a bar in Mexico City.

La Gorda and her partner in crime Calva La Tia enticed the two sportsmen to a room at the Moderno Hotel, near Garibaldi Square, in the heart of the city. Both women had been trained to steal and poison by El Hamburguesa and his wife Claudia.

The two wrestlers' cause of death was eventually defined as respiratory failure after traces of benzodiazepine were found in their bodies. This method of killing was, of course, identical to that of the gang led by El Hamburguesa until his arrest.

Months later – in July 2009 – police finally matched La Gorda's fingerprints found in the hotel room and this led detectives to her home where she was arrested. She revealed to investigators that El Hamburguesa was in fact still controlling a number of gang members from inside his prison cell.

Later, though, and for reasons unknown to anyone, La Gorda changed her story and not only denied being directly involved in the double murder of the brothers, but also claimed she had no connection to El Hamburguesa. She insisted that her accomplice Calva La Tia had administered what she thought was a light sedative to the men and they'd both fled immediately after realising the men had died.

El Hamburguesa claimed from his prison cell that the murder of the wrestlers was a copycat killing. The police believed he was lying, although they were never able to prove it conclusively. Both women were eventually each sentenced to 47 years in prison.

Two other members of El Hamburguesa's gang were each given 13-year sentences for attempted qualified homicide, skilled robbery and organised crime. More than a dozen other members of the gang were also given lengthy sentences.

By the time El Hamburguesa's trial began in October 2011, police believed the gang had been responsible for almost 100 murders, plus assaults on at least double that number of victims over a 10-year period between 1997 and 2007.

El Hamburguesa was accused in court of being personally responsible for the murder of 70 men, which made him
the third most prolific serial killer in Mexican history. He was
also alleged to be the most prolific poisoner in the country's
history, thanks to all those knockout drops administered to
victims by his 'agents'.

Despite all the allegations of mass murder against El
Hamburguesa, because prosecutors were only able to prove his
direct connection to two of the murders he was accused of incit-
ing, he was eventually sentenced to just 13 years in prison.

Mexico City police have no doubt he caused the deaths of
dozens of men. His crimes would not normally be classified
as serial killing because the murders were committed allegedly
on his orders, but following his imprisonment, criminologists
have concluded that due to the fact that he was so clearly
exorcising his own childhood demons through the murderous crimes committed on his behalf, his actions were that of a
serial killer. One with a personal and very dark motive.

CHAPTER 10

THE CARTEL ASSASSIN
JOSÉ RODRIGO ARÉCHIGA GAMBOA

Mexico's notorious Sinaloa drug cartel is one of the most lethal and successful criminal organisations on the globe. For more than three decades, they've prided themselves on the ruthlessness of their tightly knit group of criminals and were led until recently by the most infamous drug lord in Mexican history, Joaquín 'El Chapo' Guzmán.

The Sinaloa cartel's cold-blooded members are renowned for striking fear into the population to ensure that no one ever crosses them or informs on them to the authorities or their rivals. So when cartel boss Ismael 'El Mayo' Zambada gave close family friend José Rodrigo Aréchiga Gamboa a job in 2005 as a henchman inside the cartel, no one questioned Gamboa's trustworthiness.

This unlikely pair had first met after Gamboa's children became friendly with El Mayo's grandsons when they lived near each other in the cartel stronghold of Culiacán. At the time, El Mayo ran all the Sinaloa cartel's main behind-the-scenes

operations, while his co-leader 'El Chapo' Guzmán represented the more feared, public face of the organisation.

Newly recruited henchman Gamboa came from a wealthy,
educated family compared to most of the cartel's other henchmen. But he was well aware – like everyone else in Sinaloa – of
the power and influence of the cartel, which had ruled the area
with a rod of iron since the early 1980s.

Initially, Gamboa carried out day-to-day errands for
senior cartel members. New recruits were expected to show
100 per cent loyalty but most struggled at first to enforce
'rules' inside the tightly knit criminal organisation. But
Gamboa impressed the cartel because he didn't hesitate to
use violence towards those who owed money or had betrayed
the organisation.

Gamboa himself relished his new-found responsibilities
and just a few months after starting work for El Mayo, he
suggested to his boss that the cartel should set up its own hit
squad to 'take care' of all its enemies. El Mayo was at first
surprised by his young henchman's proposition, as cartels in
Mexico at that time used freelance contract killers to do their
'dirty work' for them. The narcos believed that this helped
them avoid direct links to the murderers they commissioned.
However, Gamboa convinced his boss that if the cartel had its
own gang of killers then it would actually be safer for them in
the long run because those men would be more trustworthy –
and that would mean less risk of security leaks.

El Mayo was so impressed he bounced the suggestion off cartel leader and legend El Chapo, who immediately rubber-stamped the plan. He'd always feared that the freelance killers they'd used in the past would one day inform on the cartel, and this solved the problem perfectly.

Gamboa set up an assassination bureau run for and by Sinaloa cartel gangsters. He even came up with a name for the group, calling it 'Los Ántrax' because he intended that the gang's murderous habits would be akin to a poisonous and deadly disease from which there was no cure.

Gamboa recruited a dozen criminals for his gang of hit men. Friends of his at that time later recalled him being very excited 'in a bloodthirsty way' to be heading up such an elite unit working exclusively for the cartel. El Mayo even nick-named Gamboa 'El Chino Ántrax' because of his slanty, hooded eyes, and informed Gamboa he wanted the unit of killers to also work as bodyguards for him and his family when required.

El Mayo told other cartel members he had no doubt Gamboa would make the perfect assassin. He had no criminal record, so the police didn't even have his fingerprints on file. Mexican law enforcement didn't even realise at the time that the cartel was setting up its own creed of assassins, so they could go about unsuspected.

One of Gamboa's former cartel associates later recalled: 'Gamboa believed Los Ántrax would give him a licence to kill just about anyone he wanted dead. But we didn't see it like that at all. In our minds it was just a means to an end, which would help the cartel earn even more money.'

What Gamboa's boss El Mayo and his Sinaloa cartel associates were completely unaware of was that Gamboa had already killed at least three women in Sinaloa over the previous two years, something he did after stalking and raping them. Gamboa later claimed the killings gave him a sexual thrill from the moment he began following his prey, using his honed hunting and tracking skills to shadow them, right up until he snuffed out their lives.

Back at home, Gamboa made out to his family and friends at the time that he was a high-ranking member of the Sinaloa cartel, leaving out the detail that he was the leader of a group of feral cartel killers known as Los Ántrax.

One of Gamboa's first missions with his unit of killers was to help the cartel clear all rival drug smugglers from the Mexico/US borderlands within their territory. These desolate areas were notoriously risky places to operate because of their close proximity to the US, where the police were much better equipped to crack down on narco activities.

El Mayo ordered Gamboa and his gang of killers to ensure murders were committed openly, in order to strike fear into the local population and intimidate the *gringos* on the other side of the border. Los Ántrax dumped the bodies of their first victims in public places such as pavements and parks as a chilling warning to the cartel's friends and foes not to cross them. Within weeks, bloodthirsty Gamboa and his gunmen had killed at least 20 so-called enemies of the cartel.

But the murders committed by Gamboa and Los Ántrax weren't just for the money, as far as Gamboa was concerned. He later claimed that killing all those rival criminals helped him 'stay sane', as it diverted him away from going out and killing more innocent women.

El Mayo and other senior members of the Sinaloa cartel were impressed by Los Ántrax's killing spree because it gave them an even more fearsome reputation. This reputation made it even easier for the cartel to operate with complete impunity.

Gamboa and his Los Ántrax gang were then ordered by El Mayo to begin targeting the cartel's former partners and now sworn enemies – the Beltrán-Leyva Organization and the Arellano Félix Organization. Between 2008 and 2009, Gamboa's hit men killed more than a dozen members of both these rival gangs.

He boasted to his boss El Mayo that he often pulled the trigger himself when carrying out such murders. He and his Los Ántrax thugs kidnapped gangsters from both rival groups and tortured them to get information about drug shipments before killing them. Their corpses were left hanging underneath bridges and motorway flyovers to intimidate all of the Sinaloa cartel's enemies.

When one senior cartel member suggested to El Mayo that maybe Gamboa was enjoying the killings just a little too much, El Mayo laughed and said if that was the case then that made him the perfect *sicario* (hit man).

Gamboa was on such a killing 'high' by this time that he didn't always listen properly to El Mayo's specific instructions. As a result, Gamboa's next two targets were killed before the cartel had even had a chance to torture them for information. But El Mayo resisted the temptation to reel in Gamboa's homicidal tendencies because he believed the cartel was sending out such a strong message to all their enemies, which was the main priority.

Then Gamboa and his Los Ántrax cronies shot dead two innocent people caught in the crossfire as the gang tried to assassinate one of the cartel's most notorious enemies in a busy city street.

Gamboa insisted to his boss that the deaths were just collateral damage but El Mayo and others inside the cartel feared that such indiscriminate killings of innocent people might provoke the Americans across the border to try and bring them to justice. El Mayo ordered Gamboa to slow down but refused to close down Los Ántrax for the moment, even when other cartel members criticised Gamboa's activities as being very *culichi*, which meant he was too obvious.

They claimed his killings were so blatant that many of the cartel's enemies often knew a murder was going to occur before it actually happened. That meant there was no element of surprise. El Mayo's associates also warned Gamboa that his indiscriminate killings might spark some major blowback against the cartel.

These differing opinions of Gamboa eventually caused a split inside the Sinaloa cartel between those who wanted Los Ántrax to continue and those who wanted Gamboa taken out, believing he was out of control. But Gamboa soon managed to silence the doubting voices inside the cartel. During a shoot-out known as 'The Tubutama Massacre', 29 of Gamboa's Los Ántrax assassins died in a bloody confrontation with the cartel's sworn enemy, the Beltrán-Leyva group.

Gamboa – whose reputation as 'Chino Ántrax' was by this time well known throughout the Mexican narco underworld – cleverly turned those huge manpower losses to his own advantage. He played up his own survival and proudly informed his boss El Mayo that his gang had killed more than 50 gunmen belonging to their arch enemies during the clash.

El Mayo was so impressed by fearsome Chino Ántrax that, in defiance of the doubters, he rewarded Gamboa with more power and influence inside the cartel. Unfortunately, Gamboa's promotion from henchman to full-blown narco quickly went to his head. He began hosting wild, all-night parties featuring drugs, prostitutes and live music bands. Some of the younger, more reckless Los Ántrax killers even took to social media to openly threaten their enemies. They posted photos of cars, champagne, branded clothing and footwear online, as well as showing off an array of gold-plated weapons.

'Chino Ántrax' Gamboa was rumoured to be sleeping with a different woman every night. He'd become the equivalent of an out-of-control drink-and-drug-fuelled rock star inside the cartel.

Gamboa's own family were threatened by Gamboa so many times that they became convinced he was addicted to killing. One relative later said: 'He saw murder as a "normal" thing to do and he made it clear he enjoyed doing it.'

And Gamboa's thirst for murder never faltered. When El Mayo ordered him to begin another murderous campaign against the Sinaloa cartel's enemies, he duly obliged.

Dozens more rivals were killed by Gamboa's men. Many of the murders seemed so indiscriminate to Mexican police that – under pressure from America's Drug Enforcement Administration (DEA) – they finally began taking a closer look at who exactly was carrying out the cartel's killings.

Meanwhile, senior members of the Sinaloa cartel again began voicing fears to boss El Mayo that Gamboa and his marauding gang of psychopaths were doing the organisation more harm than good. They didn't like the way Gamboa was treated by El Mayo as if he was a cartel boss, when most members considered him nothing more than a trigger-happy *sicario*, despite El Mayo's decision to promote him.

El Mayo eventually conceded that Gamboa and his band of killers needed to be reminded where their loyalties lay. So he sanctioned the hiring of outside *sicarios* (hit men) to take out several lower-ranked Los Ántrax members, to try and reduce Gamboa's growing power base inside the cartel.

Six members of Los Ántrax were shot and killed, but it ended up doing little to curtail Gamboa's ambitions, so El Mayo decided on a different tactic. He instructed his lawyers to secretly inform Mexican federal forces of Chino Ántrax's movements through a third party. It was clear by now that the cartel wanted Gamboa and his gang to be removed from the streets for ever.

The police rounded up most of Gamboa's Ántrax members but – despite police raids at numerous locations – the leader of the group was nowhere to be found.

The Sinaloa cartel's legendary leader El Chapo – in prison awaiting extradition to the US by this time – ordered El Mayo and the cartel's other bosses not to have Gamboa killed. El Chapo didn't want Gamboa alienated any further, in case he turned his guns on him and the rest of the Sinaloa cartel's top brass.

Gamboa was informed that the cartel was sparing him on condition he immediately stopped all killings, which he agreed to, much to everyone's surprise, and was bizarrely allowed to rejoin the cartel. El Mayo rewarded him with a job as chief bodyguard for his own heavily protected family in the hope it would keep him out of trouble. It seemed a risky move to many inside the cartel but El Mayo wanted to keep Gamboa close by while using his brutality to ensure his family were kept safe.

El Mayo's wife and grown-up daughter were so horrified by their new bodyguard and his reputation as a cold-blooded killer that they refused to let him protect them, though, so El Mayo relocated Gamboa, making him responsible for guarding the family's half a dozen empty homes scattered across Mexico.

Gamboa accepted the new post on condition that his boss allowed him to recruit some new henchmen to help him guard all the properties. He would need to maintain surveillance on them at all times of the day and night, and this would need resources.

He was encouraged to purchase several specially armoured trucks, which would be driven by his new gang members, and they'd use them to transport weapons and drugs between various properties and warehouses belonging to the cartel. But within weeks, Gamboa and his new team had already murdered six so-called enemies of the cartel. When confronted about the slayings, Gamboa assured El Mayo the victims had been 'spying' on El Mayo's properties and said he suspected they were about to mount an attack on the cartel.

With the overall boss El Chapo still in prison, his two adult sons, known as 'Los Chapitos', held a meeting with El Mayo to discuss how to handle the expected fallout from the killings. They'd just been informed by a corrupt police source that Gamboa was suspected of being a serial killer before he'd even joined the cartel, so the worries were mounting.

El Mayo and Los Chapitos agreed that Gamboa should be permanently removed from his post, along with all his new gang members. They just needed to track him down first.

Now on the run, Gamboa heard from one cartel member based in the US that the DEA and Mexican law enforcement had been given evidence by the cartel that directly linked him to at least a dozen narco killings. This meant, if he ever got caught, he'd never be released from prison. Gamboa immediately underwent facial plastic surgery in Mexico City before heading off on vacation to Europe, where he intended to stay until the dust had settled.

On 30 December 2013 – just one month after leaving Mexico – Gamboa flew into Amsterdam's Schiphol Airport with a new passport and a new face. But before he'd even stepped inside the airport terminal, he was surrounded by a dozen armed police officers, who'd been tipped off that he was flying into Holland.

Initially, Gamboa identified himself as Norberto Sicairos García and showed Dutch police a passport in that name. Norberto had actually been a friend of Gamboa's who had died in a recent shoot-out.

Police ignored Gamboa's lies and insisted on taking a DNA sample, which soon established his real identity. Dutch authorities then informed Gamboa that the US's DEA had asked Interpol to arrest him on charges relating to drug trafficking and murder.

In July 2014 – after more than six months of legal wrangling – Gamboa was extradited to the United States. It took almost another year after that for his trial to be held, though.

In May 2015, Gamboa pleaded guilty to charges of conspiracy to import cocaine and marijuana into the United States, admitting that he'd been a 'direct participant' in acts and threats of violence committed by the Sinaloa cartel.

The court was shown undercover photos taken by DEA agents of Gamboa in meetings with cartel boss El Mayo and another cartel member called Mayito Gordo, who was arrested three months later by the US Navy in the Gulf of Mexico.

Before Gamboa was sentenced, he told the judge he intended to work in construction and home remodelling after his eventual release.

'I'm truly ashamed. … I promise you I will never again go the wrong way. I would like to be able to work honestly.'

Gamboa then received a surprisingly short three-year custodial sentence. His Sinaloa cartel bosses immediately realised their earlier conspiracy with Mexican law enforcement officials to take Gamboa off the streets was about to blow up in their faces.

The DEA had shown Gamboa evidence that his old bosses had informed on him to authorities as an attempt to influence Gamboa into telling the Americans everything he knew about the cartel, which he did in exchange for a lighter sentence.

Back in Sinaloa, cartel chief El Mayo and others were out for revenge, but their hit men couldn't get near Gamboa because he was being guarded round the clock by DEA officers in solitary confinement in prison.

In mid 2019, Gamboa was released to complete his sentence under house arrest in San Diego, California, near the US border with Mexico.

Back in the heartlands of Mexico, El Mayo's Sinaloa cartel was by this time locked in an internal war after bosses fell out once again about how Gamboa had been handled before his arrest.

On 6 May 2020, Gamboa seemed to have the last laugh when he slipped out of the house in San Diego where he was under house arrest and disappeared into thin air. The only thing Gamboa left behind was his mobile phone.

It became known that he had travelled back over the border to Mexico, to be reunited with his family. Sinaloa cartel members immediately received reports of sightings of Gamboa in their stronghold of Culiacán, where he had once struck fear and loathing into the population as the psycho-killer head of Los Ántrax. The Sinaloa cartel not only wanted revenge on Gamboa for being an informant but they were also convinced he'd duped them into setting up his gang of murderers in order to satisfy his own serial killing urges.

Within hours of Gamboa being sighted in Culiacán, a dozen hand-picked Sinaloa cartel henchmen burst into Gamboa's sister's house where they knew he was hiding.

Gamboa, his sister and her husband were all dragged out of the house and taken away in a fleet of trucks.

The bodies of all three were discovered the following day in Gamboa's sister's burned-out black SUV parked on the outskirts of Culiacán. There was no sign of a GPS tag that should have been on Gamboa's leg as part of the condition of his house arrest. But one cartel insider later revealed that US law enforcement authorities had been monitoring all Gamboa's movements from the moment he left his house in San Diego, thanks to that tag.

Despite initial denials that Gamboa had been a DEA informant, US law enforcement later admitted that Gamboa had helped them discover and then destroy at least two cocaine 'factories' in the desert. What role he played in the downfall of El Chapo will probably never be fully known.

A photo was later leaked on social media of Gamboa's bullet-riddled corpse. While it clearly showed the marks of his facial plastic surgery, and to all intents and purposes was him, it was pointed out at the time that narcos often fake their deaths, and have done so frequently in the past, so we may never fully know.

But what we do know is the trail of victims he left behind. One former cartel member later said: 'The guy was a monster. He was a serial killer, not a professional assassin. It's clear he only ever formed the Ántrax gang to satisfy his own lust for murder. We had to get rid of him once and for all before he did any further harm to our business. But I can assure you, Gamboa will never rise again from the dead, thank God.'

One Mexican law enforcement officer explained: 'Gamboa wasn't just another narco killer. He had the blood of many innocent people on his hands.'

CHAPTER 11

THE MONSTERS OF ECATEPEC
JUAN CARLOS HERNÁNDEZ
AND PATRICIA MARTINEZ

The coastal town of Lázaro Cárdenas, Michoacán, was a classic working community in the heartlands of Mexico. It had a bustling town plaza filled with beggars and street vendors and most weekends locals would fill the bars and clubs.

Many men had their girlfriends or wives squeezed in next to them in their pickup trucks as they coasted around the plaza, admiring other women on the pavement. But just beyond that same plaza were some less well lit, shadowy, narrow streets that most hard-working families avoided because of the hustlers and thieves hiding in there.

Down one of those alleyways was a bar with a bright neon lit sign outside it that simply said 'Club'. A lot of men visited these premises late at night, often after drinking heavily at the better-known bars on the main square. Inside the 'Club' was a long, dimly lit bar with at least a dozen women sitting on stools, examining every man who walked in.

One of these customers was a shy 17-year-old called Juan Carlos Hernández. He'd only gone in there on a Saturday night in the summer of 2003 out of curiosity after someone had told him the women were surprisingly pretty. Within moments, he'd noticed a girl in her early twenties that he really liked the look of. But Juan Carlos struggled to catch the eye of the girl, so he downed his beer and walked out, looking down at the floor as he left so as not to catch the eyes of the other women who kept asking him to stop and talk to them.

Fifty yards down the same narrow, darkened road, Juan Carlos stopped for a moment to light a cigarette. He turned and glanced back at the gaudy pink-rimmed neon lit sign of the same club as it flickered in the darkness. After finishing his cigarette, he threw it on the ground, stamped it out and began heading back towards the bar. He was determined to talk to that same girl he'd seen earlier, but the other women backed away from him immediately, having worked out who he was really interested in.

When Juan Carlos caught the eye of the girl, she smiled. She had noticed him earlier but decided he was too young for her. In any case, he probably didn't have any money, so she had turned her attention to another, older man. But this time, Juan Carlos plucked up the courage to approach her. She greeted him as if they were old friends and took his hand to guide him to the darker end of the bar, where she stopped and asked him to buy her a drink. She knew the manager was watching through the two-way mirror overlooking them, as there was a strict rule that the girls had to get the men to buy them a drink before there was any attempt to negotiate a fee for having sex with them.

After Juan Carlos had bought her an overpriced glass of fake champagne and himself a beer, she pulled him by the hand on to the dance floor. He was much more reticent than most men, who'd either grab the women and grunt 'how much' or nod towards the stairs up to the bedrooms before they'd even paid for a drink.

All the women who worked in the bar knew they weren't permitted to spend more than five minutes on the dance floor with a customer, otherwise the manager would send one of his henchmen to talk to them about not doing their job properly. So the girl whispered in Juan Carlos's ear as they danced that they needed to go up to her room. He hesitated for a moment because he wasn't sure that was really what he wanted.

She smiled at his shyness, tilted her head and carried on dancing to give him a chance to absorb what she'd just said to him. Across the bar, two other women winked at the girl, knowing that this younger man clearly fancied her and that it was just a matter of time.

Then, instead of asking 'how much', Juan Carlos whispered in her ear.

'What's your name?'

She answered 'Patricia', took hold of his hand gently and they walked towards the staircase next to the dance floor.

Once they got into the room a few minutes later, Patricia Martínez Bernal patted the bed next to her and urged Juan Carlos to sit down and talk to her. He was relieved because it didn't feel as strange as he'd expected.

After chatting for at least 10 minutes, they kissed briefly before she urged him to leave her room, as she knew the manager would soon be knocking for his share of the money she was supposed to have charged Juan Carlos for sex. Juan Carlos hesitated to leave until Patricia warned him that she would be in trouble if he didn't go immediately. They agreed to meet the following afternoon when she was 'off duty'.

After he'd gone, Patricia removed some cash from inside the drawer of her tatty bedside table to give to the manager, so he'd think she slept with Juan Carlos. For the first time in Patricia's brief and troubled life, she felt as if she'd done something good. The boy was a bit younger than her but, unsure if she was imagining it, he seemed to genuinely want a proper relationship with her.

The following afternoon, Juan Carlos met Patricia in the town square. Patricia looked embarrassed each time she noticed the smirks from some of the men who walked past them with their wives and children. Juan Carlos was so infatuated with her, he didn't even see the expressions on the other men's faces.

The couple eventually sat down at a cafe and talked so intensely for such a long period of time that they forgot to drink their coffees. They discovered they'd been born on the same day six years apart in Lázaro Cárdenas. Juan Carlos explained to Patricia how his mother had raised him on her own when his father walked out on them. She nodded and said it must have been hard for his mother, which was true.

Juan Carlos had always struggled to make ordinary conversation with anyone but it seemed much easier with Patricia. He told Patricia how his mother had been so disappointed not to have had a girl that sometimes she made him wear a dress when he was little. This usually happened when his mother brought men to their house and made him watch them having sex.

Juan Carlos was surprised and relieved when she didn't seem shocked when he said that. And when she asked him why he agreed to wear a dress, he answered simply: 'To make my mother happy because she always seemed so sad.'

Patricia later recalled that she thought about his reply for a few moments before taking his hand and kissing him gently on the lips. She sensed, correctly, that he'd never told anyone else about what had happened to him.

Juan Carlos didn't even question why he was telling this girl everything. None of his worries seemed to matter because he'd already decided she was 'the one'. Patricia nodded slowly as Juan Carlos unloaded everything on to her and kept assuring him it made no difference to the way she felt about him.

Juan Carlos went on to confess to Patricia how during his childhood he'd also been sexually abused by an older woman who'd looked after him at home when his mother was out at work. It had happened when he was just 10 years old. He told Patricia he'd been so upset that he'd tried to get away from the woman and accidentally fell down the stairs at his home. The injuries he suffered resulted in a lengthy stay in hospital.

Patricia suggested that perhaps Juan Carlos had actually been trying to commit suicide. He conceded that was probably true and also said that when he was finally discharged from hospital, he'd felt like a completely different person from before.

He said he'd become much colder and more distant, and that he'd started to truly hate his mother and had decided he didn't really care what happened to her. Patricia nodded patiently as he spoke because she knew what it was like to be abused during childhood. She told Juan Carlos how she'd been born into a poor family and had been physically and sexually abused since the age of six by some of her mother's male friends.

She'd endured the abuse for at least two years until she began running away from home, knowing it was the only way to escape the attacks. However, each time she left, she was tracked down by a relative and forcibly returned to her mother, who would scold her for daring to run away and then force her to sleep with yet another one of her male friends.

Just before her 13th birthday, Patricia left home for good and headed as far away as possible in the hope no one would ever find her. But in order to survive, she'd ended up working in the very same brothel where Juan Carlos had just met her.

After Patricia had finished, Juan Carlos asked her how old she was and she replied: 'Nineteen.' Really, she was four years older than that. Patricia later recalled that she fell in love with Juan Carlos that afternoon as they poured everything out to each other.

She explained: 'He knew I was sleeping with strangers for money but he still respected me because he knew I had no choice in the matter. I just hoped and prayed he'd be the first man I'd ever had a relationship with who didn't hit me.'

That same afternoon Juan Carlos also confessed to Patricia about his own career as a petty criminal breaking into houses and robbing motorists on deserted streets. His crimes had almost landed him in jail on several occasions and he'd been worried it might put her off him. But it actually made her even more attracted to him, Patricia assured Juan Carlos.

Although they didn't realise it at the time, both of them suffered from borderline intelligence disorders which meant they often lacked normal emotional responses to certain situations. This mental illness had made Patricia extremely submissive, especially if she was afraid someone was going to reject her. That afternoon, Juan Carlos walked Patricia back to the brothel and tried his hardest not to think about what she was about to do for the rest of the evening.

Over the following few weeks, they met up for several more platonic afternoon dates. In their conversations, Patricia made it clear she couldn't afford not to work in the brothel and Juan Carlos had no choice but to agree, at least for the moment.

The couple eventually slept together in a room at a local motel. They both admitted afterwards it was awkward and not very satisfying, as each of them found it hard not to think about the suffering they'd been through. But there was another reason why Patricia found having normal, loving sex so difficult.

Some of the male customers at the brothel paid her to beat them and she'd discovered that inflicting pain on them provided her with an emotional escape hatch by helping her satisfy her deep-set hatred of most men. But Patricia didn't want to tell Juan Carlos any of this before she'd more fully explored that part of her sexuality.

Then one day, as they were about to make love in another cheap hotel room, Patricia asked Juan Carlos outright if he'd ever hurt someone. He didn't know what she meant at first. He was six years younger than her, so in some ways he was still very naive. But when Patricia pressed him further, he nervously asked her to tell him why she'd asked that question.

Patricia paused for a few moments before explaining to him in vivid detail about how she fantasised about murdering the men she slept with for money. Juan Carlos surprised even himself by not being shocked by what she told him. He'd noticed Patricia's breathing became very uneven as she spoke but he wasn't sure if it was down to being nervous or excited by what she was explaining.

And that night they had the best sex they'd ever experienced. Juan Carlos told one of his few friends at the time that he was sure he'd found the love of his life.

Patricia was equally smitten but made a point of telling Juan Carlos she expected him to make love to her each and every night. And if he didn't, then she'd presume he had another lover and would kill him. He wasn't sure if she was joking.

Soon afterwards, the couple decided to move in together but agreed they should live in Mexico City where there was more chance of proper work. They ended up in the dirt-poor suburb of Ecatepec.

Juan Carlos was so relieved that Patricia had finally stopped working in the brothel that he pledged that he would work to support them both. She was relieved to have an opportunity for a 'normal life' and suggested they set up a business together once they'd settled in Mexico City.

Over the following seven years, this most unlikely pair of lovers had four children and seemed, to friends and family, to be a genuinely happy couple. Along the way, they opened a business selling clothing, perfume and mobile phones from the modest house where they lived with their children in Ecatepec.

As the business expanded, they recruited staff to work in a warehouse where they stored all their goods. Patricia noticed that Juan Carlos often hired attractive women who were much younger than both of them.

So when one of the women they'd employed told her that Juan Carlos had tried to have sex with her, Patricia got extremely angry with him and threatened to walk out on him. He broke down and begged her to reconsider, though he never actually denied the woman's allegations. Juan Carlos also pointed out to Patricia that they'd hardly had sex since the birth of their youngest child, so it wouldn't have been such a big surprise if he'd started 'looking elsewhere'.

Patricia looked Juan Carlos right in the eye for a few moments then ordered him to 'go out and find yourself a whore'. She surprised him even more by adding that she expected her husband to 'share his conquests' with her. Juan Carlos wasn't completely sure what Patricia meant and feared she might be testing him out, so for the following few months he was very careful not to do anything more to upset her.

Later, Patricia recalled how the notion of them both sharing the same woman turned her on and she began pressing him to find them such a person. She also explained to him that 'certain things' needed to happen to those women, otherwise she wouldn't permit him to bring any of them home.

At first, Juan Carlos was confused by her demands but then it dawned on him that he could do anything he wanted if he did it her way. Juan Carlos said it felt to him as if Patricia was throwing down the gauntlet to him. She also warned him that if he didn't get a woman soon then she'd go out and find a man just for herself.

A few days later – in the early summer of 2012 – Juan Carlos brought a 22-year-old woman back to their house to interview her for a job at the couple's warehouse. Patricia later recalled that on that day she was so exhausted from looking after their four children that she barely looked up when her husband walked in with the woman. When two of the children began crying, she told her husband that they'd go into the yard while he interviewed the woman, given it was so noisy in the house.

Just after they'd all left, the woman asked Juan Carlos where the bathroom was. He politely insisted on showing her and even opened the door for her.

As she entered, he suddenly pushed her to the floor and locked the door from the inside. Then he shoved his hand over her mouth and began ripping off her clothing. When Patricia heard the woman's muffled screams from outside, she ushered their children round to the front of the house, so they couldn't hear the noise so clearly.

Back inside the bathroom, Juan Carlos looked down at the woman who was now lying curled up on the tiled floor in floods of tears. He leaned down and punched her repeatedly in the face until she lost consciousness. Then he dragged her limp body into the shower.

Standing over her, Juan Carlos studied her bruised and bloodied body for a few moments before pulling out a knife from a sheath attached to his belt. Then, as she began to stir, he crouched down and pressed the tip of the blade into the side of her neck.

Once she'd opened her eyes, he sank the knife deep into her neck and twisted the handle until he could hear her lungs crackling as she tried to scream. He then pulled the handle of the knife under her chin and round towards her ear until he'd beheaded her. Juan Carlos stood up, calmly turned on the shower tap and watched as the water flushed away most of the blood around the woman's torso and head down the drain.

Just a few yards away, Patricia and the couple's four young children were sitting on a kerb on the dusty street. She wasn't sure what to do next but she could tell something must have happened and wanted to be out of the house.

Back in the bathroom, Juan Carlos cleaned his knife on a towel before cutting the body up into manageable pieces. He placed the parts in three white plastic shopping bags and then calmly opened the bathroom window, leaned out and told Patricia and the children to come back into the house.

Juan Carlos carried all three shopping bags into the kitchen as Patricia filled three large cooking pots with hot water from a kettle. They'd discussed what would happen to the women many times before, so she knew what was in the bags. She'd even been the one who'd earlier left the plastic bags in the bathroom so he could use them.

She turned and nodded knowingly towards Juan Carlos as he began taking each body part out of the bag, which he then dropped into the hot water with a soft plop.

As the pots slowly simmered on the cooker, Patricia poured some beans on to four plates from another saucepan and put them in front of her children. She ordered them to hurry up and eat their supper because it was time for bed. A few minutes later, Juan Carlos sat on the edge of the family's only bed, opened a book and read his four children a story before tucking them in and kissing them goodnight.

Back in the kitchen, Patricia was casually sprinkling some light seasoning into each of the stewing pots while they simmered on the cooker. She then laid two places on the kitchen table for her and Juan Carlos and sliced up some home-baked bread on a wooden board, to dip in their stew.

Neither Juan Carlos nor Patricia said much when they finally sat down to eat together, but she later recalled that was mainly because they were so hungry that they didn't have time to talk.

Accounts vary, but Patricia later insisted that eating the remains of that young woman had been Juan Carlos's idea. He wanted them to 'share' another person, even though they hadn't both slept with their victim as they'd planned.

She claimed that when she first realised he'd murdered the woman, she wanted to call the police, but Juan Carlos had then warned her that they'd both be locked up and their children put in care, so she agreed not to tell anyone what had happened.

Juan Carlos later admitted he believed he was a 'demon' and needed to drink human blood and eat human flesh on a regular basis. He insisted that he'd planned for them both to sleep with her first but then he found himself compelled to kill her immediately.

However, it was later alleged that Patricia had in fact encouraged Juan Carlos to kill the woman on condition they consumed her together. It was claimed that she found it sexually exciting to know what he'd done to her.

Juan Carlos later sold the woman's bones to a local Santería priest so they could be used in black magic ceremonies. But whatever the truth of the matter, this twisted murder altered the direction of both their lives for ever. Psychological experts believe the couple felt they'd been liberated by carrying out the killing in that it proved to one another that they could share everything, even the flesh of another human being.

Patricia later admitted that following the first murder, she urged Juan Carlos to lure more women into their home so they could be killed and then eaten because she liked him doing it. In any case, it was their secret and having that secret made them both feel even more empowered.

The couple then began placing advertisements in local newspapers looking for housekeepers to work in their home. They knew that the women who would respond would mostly be desperate for money and would presume they were safe because a woman – Patricia – was present in the house.

All the women who visited the couple's house would end up being raped and killed by Juan Carlos or sometimes Patricia. She later admitted stabbing at least two of the victims to death herself.

Following each murder, Juan Carlos would perform the same type of 'ritual' as with their first victim by dismembering the remains in the shower. Then he'd cut the torso into pieces and slice the meat from the bones before presenting Patricia with a minimum of a kilo of 'steaks' from each victim.

Having boiled the remains after that first killing, the couple decided the meat would be much tastier if they fried it, rather than try and soften it up in a slow-cooking stew. Patricia was always in charge of turning the 'steaks' in a pan to ensure they were properly cooked and tender. She would usually added tomatoes and chilli oil to enhance the taste.

Any leftover organs of each victim were chopped up and fed to the family's two dogs. Other human parts were dropped into buckets of specially prepared wet concrete that would quickly solidify in the backyard.

As their addiction to killing and eating their victims grew, they began leaving shorter gaps between kills. When one of the family dogs ate the remains of the heart of one victim, just before they'd planned to put it in a bag to offer to the local black magic priest, the couple become convinced a curse would be put on them, so they immediately lured another victim into the family home, killed her and dispatched her heart to the priest instead.

When they ran out of women to come to the house for job interviews, the couple decided their sixth should be a teenage girl who lived next door to them in the barrio. She was a glue addict and the couple persuaded her to come and babysit for their children while they supposedly went out for dinner.

Minutes before the girl was due to arrive, Patricia ushered their four children into the yard behind the house, so she could keep watch on her neighbours – the girl's parents – in case they came out looking for the child after she disappeared.

Moments after the girl knocked on the front door, Juan Carlos answered and showed her into the house, where he handcuffed her and gagged her. Then he dragged her into the bathroom while his children played in the yard outside with mother Patricia.

Juan Carlos raped the teenager in the bathroom and then beheaded her before dismembering her body in the shower. Less than half an hour later, Patricia was mincing up the remains of their latest victim before turning it into a chilli con carne, which the couple devoured after the children had been put to bed.

The disappearance of young women in Ecatepec got very little media and police coverage as people were constantly disappearing from the streets of the poverty-stricken slum. Relatives of the victims accused the police of not really caring about their missing loved ones. Juan Carlos and Patricia were surprised there seemed to be no public interest in their victims and were convinced they'd be able to get away with more murders.

Over the following six years between 2012 and 2018, at least a dozen more women and girls disappeared in Ecatepec. Police blamed most of the disappearances on the area's high crime rate and issued a warning that the streets of Ecatepec were especially dangerous for women out on their own. It sounded to many like an excuse for the failure of law enforcement to properly investigate the disappearances.

One Mexico City newspaper disclosed at the time that Ecatepec had the highest femicide rate in the entire nation. The police responded by issuing a statement that this was why they hadn't been able to trace the missing women. They called it an epidemic of murder.

The heartbroken relatives of Juan Carlos and Patricia's victims became so infuriated by the police's failure to find their loved ones that some mothers formed an action group to launch their own investigation into the women's movements on the days they disappeared.

These mothers quickly established that three of the missing women – including one who'd disappeared with her two-month-old daughter – had the phone number of Patricia Martínez Bernal on their mobile phones.

The mothers discovered that Patricia lived with her boyfriend, Juan Carlos Hernández, and their four children in the same neighbourhood where all the women had gone missing. The couple lived right next to the family of one girl who'd disappeared.

The mothers also discovered that the parents of one missing 13-year-old girl had let Juan Carlos and Patricia and their children live with them for a few months when their home was being renovated. The teenage girl in question had disappeared a few weeks after Patricia and Juan Carlos had moved back into the house.

When Juan Carlos and Patricia were confronted by the mothers of the missing girls, the couple immediately blamed another neighbour for the schoolgirl's disappearance. But the mothers weren't convinced and took all their suspicions back to the police.

In early October 2018, the police finally acknowledged they could no longer ignore the missing women's relatives. They launched a surveillance operation on the home of Juan Carlos and Patricia.

Three days later, the police arrived late for a morning surveillance session and missed a woman and her seven-year-old daughter turning up at the house and entering through the front door.

Inside the property, Patricia and Juan Carlos had instantly overpowered the child and her mother. Juan Carlos later claimed he hadn't planned to harm the little girl and that her mother was their intended target. The couple had no idea their home was being monitored by the police at the time.

Juan Carlos and Patricia kept the child and her mother hidden for a week in the basement of their home, despite the police surveillance team watching their house most of the time. Then on the seventh day, Juan Carlos strangled both the mother and child. He never explained why he killed them and even insisted later to investigators that he did not sexually abuse either of them.

Patricia later recalled that she told Juan Carlos after this double killing that they needed to stop, believing it would only be a matter of time before they were caught. She claimed that Juan Carlos ignored her.

Their next victim was a young mother called Noemí Huitrón who went missing with her baby daughter in late September 2017. Again, for some unknown reason, the police surveillance team did not see them enter the house.

After Noemí's murder, Juan Carlos and Patricia sold the infant to another couple for 15,000 pesos through an illegal adoption network. They'd claimed Patricia had given birth to the baby, but that they couldn't afford to keep her.

On 4 October 2017 – more than a week after Patricia and Juan Carlos had lured that mother and baby into their home – they were spotted by the police surveillance team leaving their home. Patricia was pushing a baby stroller.

Officers had no idea about the latest murder victim Noemí and her child but believed that the neighbour's missing daughter was still being held prisoner inside the property.

Thus, more than a dozen officers swarmed into the front yard of the house and stopped the couple.

When Patricia looked awkwardly down at the stroller, one of the policeman pulled a blanket off it and noticed something wrapped tightly in black plastic. He leaned down and used a penknife to carefully slice open the package. Before he'd even finished peeling off the outer layer of plastic, the policeman could see the mottled skin of a child's torso.

Patricia and Juan Carlos were immediately arrested. As they were being escorted to a waiting van, other officers started searching the couple's house and a nearby vacant lot that they owned. They eventually uncovered eight large plastic buckets filled with concrete in the backyard. Human organs were found encased in each one.

Back inside the couple's home, investigators opened the refrigerator and discovered human remains wrapped in plastic. A subsequent forensic examination later established that the body parts belonged to eight different women, although subsequent DNA tests led to only four of them being properly identified.

Noemí's baby daughter was found safe and returned to her maternal grandmother. The couple who purchased her were arrested on human trafficking charges.

Juan Carlos eventually gave investigators detailed accounts of 10 murders the couple had committed. He also told them that they'd killed a further 10 people but he wasn't able to identify them.

Prosecutors and police were so stunned by the large numbers of murders that at first they thought Juan Carlos was more a fantasist than a serial killer. As one prosecutor said at the time: 'He just seemed so proud to have done this. He wanted people to see his picture, to know his name … at first we thought he might be making it all up but it soon became clear he wasn't.'

Inside the couple's two properties, police also discovered articles of clothing, many of which belonged to their victims.

Across Mexico, there was anger that the police had been so slow to react to the disappearances of so many women. More than 1,000 people marched through the streets of Ecatepec, demanding justice for the victims and attacking the police for not protecting law-abiding citizens from the killer couple and crime in general.

As the details of their heinous crimes were publicised throughout the world, the media dubbed the couple 'The Monsters of Ecatepec'.

One psychologist who examined Juan Carlos before his trial told prosecutors he had some type of schizoid disorder. Juan Carlos told the same expert how his mother had been both physically and emotionally abusive towards him, and about the female caregiver who'd sexually molested him when he was a child.

Juan Carlos also revealed that his mother had worked as a prostitute when he was a child and that was when she'd force him to watch her have sex with men. That was why, he later explained, he hated women so much. He said: 'I'd rather my little dogs ate the victims' organs than for them (the women) to keep breathing oxygen.'

Despite questions over their mental health, the court ruled that the couple still knew right from wrong and were therefore fit to stand trial. Under Mexican justice rules, Juan Carlos and Patricia were supposed to stand trial separately for the murder of each of the eight victims, which state prosecutors felt confident enough to prove them guilty of.

At the trial for the first murder, Juan Carlos and Patricia spent much of the time whispering and giggling in each other's ears, even as graphic details of their murders were disclosed in open court for the first time. Relatives of their victims were appalled that the couple gave the impression they were not taking their murder trial seriously. No one in court was surprised when the judge found the couple guilty and sentenced them to life in prison for their first murder.

Following this – between April and October of 2019 – the couple stood trial several more times on charges of femicide, hiding human remains for the purpose of concealing a crime, and human trafficking for selling Noemi's infant daughter illegally.

Juan Carlos and Patricia were eventually sentenced to a total of 327 years each in prison. They were never able to explain what really drove them to kill and then eat so many innocent people apart from their twisted desire to share the victims with each other.

Women's rights groups hailed the 2019 trial of the couple as having helped to expose the large number of women being murdered in Mexico and how few of their killers ever face justice, as the police so rarely try hard enough to track them down. It's estimated by UN Women that in the previous year – 2018 – a total of seven women and girls were being killed throughout Mexico every day.

Mexico State – where Ecatepec is located – led the country in femicides in that same year of 2018, with 301 women and girls murdered, according to official figures.

Across Mexico as a whole in 2018, there were 28,702 murders, more than any previous year. This was at the same time the government deployed multiple army units to wage war on the country's violent and powerful drug cartels, an action that clearly diverted many law enforcement officers from investigating other types of serious crime, including the murders committed by this couple. A couple who perhaps could have been stopped sooner.

EPILOGUE:
SICARIA SERIAL KILLERS

The serial-killing epidemic sweeping through Mexico is so huge that it was impossible to cover all of these heinous crimes in detail in this book. An exceptionally large number of them have crossed the line between narcos and serial killings, so it's imperative to mention the rest of the most shocking ones here, albeit briefly.

Many Mexican criminals claim there is a clear distinction between these types of murders because the cartel sicarios (hit men) kill professionally. But at the end of the day, what they have committed is mass murder, whatever way you try to dress it up.

Killing in the name of a drug cartel does not disqualify some-one from being a serial killer.

Mexican crime experts estimate that at least 50 per cent of this nation's marauding narco gangland executors are self-motivated psychopaths out to satisfy their own lust for blood and death. And the prevalence of these types of killers shows no sign of slowing down either.

Enrique Aurelio Elizondo Flores, variously called 'El Arabe' ('The Arab') or 'The Raven', confessed in 2021 to the murders of at least 75 people on behalf of the Los Zetas drug cartel.

Flores and his crew of gunmen often stopped buses travelling to the Texan border and lined passengers up and shot dozens of them dead just to send a message to his cartel's enemies. Flores revelled so much in this ongoing bloodshed that he often recorded himself on a video camera mutilating the bodies of several of his victims.

One clip of mobile phone footage shows a smiling Flores dancing to reggae music with his associates at the same time as he slices the ears and fingers off corpses. In the background, more human fingers and the ears of the victims could clearly be seen in a plastic shopping bag.

When Flores was asked if he was sorry for the slaughters he'd taken part in, he replied: 'I only regret having killed those who were innocent and women.'

Several of the most powerful Mexican drug cartels use female contract killers as their executioners. These so-called *sicarias* are so bloodthirsty that criminologists say they also qualify as serial killers.

A significant percentage of the most notorious hit women in Mexico have openly admitted they used the drug business as an excuse to get revenge on men for hurting them in the past. Given the singularity of these motives, we can almost certainly class these femmes fatales as serial killers.

'A lot of these women are psychologically damaged almost beyond repair,' explained one Mexican criminologist. 'Some even volunteer as professional killers for the narcos to get back at men because of the way they've been treated by them.

'Men who kill for the cartels seem able to detach themselves from the emotion of what they do while women literally revel in it.'

One *sicaria* admitted recently that she always tried to look her best when she carried out a hit, as she liked the way her male targets thought she found them attractive just moments before she snuffed out their lives.

Most of these *sicaria* killers are in their twenties, though this is probably because few of these women live past thirty.

The notorious head of the Sinaloa drug cartel Joaquín 'El Chapo' Guzmán appointed a woman called Claudia Ochoa Felix as his number one *sicaria* before he was rearrested and ended up in a US prison in 2016.

She was dubbed the 'Kim Kardashian of the Narcos' in the Mexican media. Having allegedly killed more than 50 male enemies of the Sinaloa cartel, she was found dead in her lover's bed from what doctors called 'a pulmonary aspiration'. Many presume it was caused by someone choking her to death.

Other female executioners inside the cartels flaunt their bloodthirsty lifestyles on social media, posing with guns, flak jackets and even tigers in a bid to show off their wealth, power and influence inside the Mexican drug underworld.

One of the cartels' most fearsome *sicarias* was a former sex worker called Juana reputed to have murdered dozens of men. She was known as 'Le Peque' or 'The Little One'. Born in Hidalgo, near Mexico City, she first met members of the ruthless Los Zetas cartel while working as a prostitute.

The Little One later explained: 'I was being abused by men every night and then there was this opportunity to leave the brothel and get revenge on them. It was a no-brainer. In any case, I had children to support.'

The Little One began her narcos career as a lookout for the Zetas on the streets of her home city of Nuevo Laredo, Tamaulipas. She kept watch for their enemies and police patrols for up to eight hours a day and became one of the cartel's most trusted informants.

One day, The Little One witnessed a man's head being smashed with a mace during a torture session. She later claimed she was horrified but didn't show her emotions to the men who'd done it.

The Little One explained: 'I remember feeling sad and thinking I did not want to end up like that, but I knew I had to keep those feelings to myself. I learned to hide my emotions even more than when I worked in a brothel.'

Her male cartel bosses were so impressed by The Little One's chilling attitude towards death that they offered her work as a *sicaria*. The money was 20 times more than she'd been earning as a sex worker. She later explained that the first few killings she carried out were relatively easy and she soon began to realise she was enjoying shooting men dead.

'I felt immense satisfaction at ending some nasty man's life. It felt like payback time after all those years of abuse in the brothel,' she explained.

However, The Little One also knew that if she ever crossed her cartel bosses she'd most likely be raped and then tied up and left in a warehouse for days and possibly even killed as punishment.

When The Little One's fourth victim fell to the floor after she'd shot him dead, she found herself fixated by the blood gushing from his wounds.

'I couldn't take my eyes off it,' she later explained. 'I just stood there shaking with excitement.'

The Little One claimed she then smeared some of that victim's blood on herself as she stood over his body. After that, she drained some of the blood into a cup before leaving the scene of the shooting. Moments later – after getting in her car – she drank it all.

'It was still warm and I remember being in such ecstasy. I masturbated as I sat there in the driver's seat,' she recalled.

Each time The Little One carried out another killing, she took larger quantities of her victim's blood and even started to bathe in it, as well as drinking it.

She later admitted: 'I was in such a state of feverish excitement every time I completed a kill that I'd lost touch with reality.'

The Little One sometimes stopped her male cartel associates from dismembering a victim so she could have sex with the corpse first. She later claimed that on one occasion she straddled a headless body. Her reign of terror came to an end with her arrest in 2016. When one investigator accused her of being a serial killer, she shrugged her shoulders and just said: 'Sure. Why not.'

Another notorious serial-killing *sicaria* was Joselyn Alejandra Niño known as 'La Flaca' – meaning 'The Skinny One'. She posted photos of herself online dressed in a bulletproof vest and displaying a tattoo with her surname emblazoned across her chest.

In 2015, La Flaca worked as an assassin for the Los Ciclones cartel, a splinter group of the notoriously powerful Gulf Cartel, who were in the midst of a violent turf war with rival narcos just south of the Mexican border with Texas.

La Flaca was credited with at least a dozen hits over a period of two months before an abandoned truck was found in a car park in the city of Matamoros. It contained three blue-and-white beer coolers in the flatbed. In one of them, police found a bare right foot and a woman's right arm with a tattoo reading 'Niño'. La Flaca's murder-for-hire activities had finally caught up with her.

* * *

The large number of individuals who have got away with committing serial killings for decades with impunity in Mexico highlights failings by the country's judicial service.

Mexico prioritises the imprisonment of offenders rather than effective forms of rehabilitation that could help those same inmates to not offend again. As a result, experts today are convinced that some criminals currently incarcerated in this nation's jails could evolve into dangerous people, even serial killers, when they're released from prison.

A lack of psychological evaluation and treatment for mental health issues means these ex-inmates could slip through the system and end up becoming serial killers as has happened many times in the past.

The themes running through the stories of the *Serial Killers of Mexico* provide an undeniable link between sex and violence. Traumatic experiences during childhood seem to have turned certain individuals into serial killers.

But acknowledging this isn't enough in itself to prevent more mass murders or help bring existing psychopaths to justice.

And it will never help bring the victims of serial killers back to life either.

ACKNOWLEDGEMENTS

To all the law enforcement agents who helped me with this book – both still serving and now retired – I offer my eternal thanks.

I would also like to thank the experts who've helped me try to provide at least some of the answers as to how and why these serial killers murdered in the first place.